HAUNTS OF SAN JOSE

CALIFORNIA

David Lee

Schiffer Publishing Ltd

4880 Lower Valley Road, Atglen, Pennsylvania 19310

Schiffer Books are
available at special discounts
for bulk purchases for sales promotions or
premiums. Special editions, including personalized
covers, corporate imprints, and excerpts can be
created in large quantities for special needs. For
more information contact the publisher:

Schiffer Publishing Ltd.
4880 Lower Valley Road
Atglen, PA 19310
Phone: (610) 593-1777; Fax: (610) 593-2002
E-mail: Info@schifferbooks.com

Please visit our web site catalog at
www.schifferbooks.com

We are always looking for people to write books on
new and related subjects. If you have an idea for a
book, please contact us at the above address.

This book may be purchased from the publisher.
Include $5.00 for shipping. Please try your
bookstore first. You may write for a free catalog.

In Europe, Schiffer books are distributed by:
Bushwood Books
6 Marksbury Ave.
Kew Gardens
Surrey TW9 4JF, England
Phone: 44 (0)208 392-8585
Fax: 44 (0)208 392-9876
E-mail: Info@bushwoodbooks.co.uk

Website: www.bushwoodbooks.co.uk
Free postage in the UK. Europe: air mail at
cost. Please try your bookstore first

ACKNOWLEDGEMENTS

Many people have helped me out and this book would not exist without their contributions. Ron Bricmont and Ray Castillo at Grant Ranch, Tu Tran, David Derr, Shadowlands.net, Denise Padia, Henry Jacobo, Greg Woods, Johnny Johnson, Norma, Connie, and Gloria Ortiz, Susan Sablan, Brian Glenn, Petra Wright, Norman Canady, Sergio Perez, David Howard, Cathy Zitzer, Mary Romesberg, Isabel and Junior Ramirez, George Kahwaty, Valentine Granado, Bill Wulf, Dinah Roseberry, Sheryl Boissiere, and everyone one else—although unnamed, not forgotten.

CONTENTS

INTRODUCTION

More than one million people live in the city of San Jose, and this city *definitely* has its share of ghosts. San Jose was originally the capitol of California, and the numerous Indian burial grounds existing throughout the town have certainly contributed to the number of ghosts and spirits residing there. When people die, a tremendous amount of energy is released into the atmosphere. This energy is a duplicate of the person who died. Most ghosts may not be able to materialize because they do not have enough energy required to do so. But there are ghosts and spirits that are capable of materializing completely because energy equals mass. The human energy collects and condenses into a solid person. *Haunts of San Jose* is the result of an extensive quest for information I gathered from one end of the city to the other. As soon as a ghost or spirit enters your household, you have little or no secrets you can hide from these invisible visitors.

Chapter One:
ENTITIES
OF EAST SAN JOSE

NEAR BERRYESSA ROAD...AND TEXAS!

Petra Wright was resting on the couch at her mother's house located near Berryessa Road. Her mom's pet Chihuahua was barking incessantly, and Petra wondered what was bothering the dog. The blanket Petra was using was not covering her feet and she felt the hand of a ghost touching her foot.

Immediately alarmed, she looked around the room to see what was going on. In the hallway mirror, visible from where she sat, was the reflection of the ghost of a woman wearing a dress. The ghost was slowly floating up and down before making her way from the living room to the kitchen. Petra followed the ghost down the hallway, through the kitchen, into the dining room, and out the back door where the ghost disappeared in the backyard.

Petra's mom never met her father who died in Texas. Petra's mom encountered the ghost of a man wearing a hat. He walked by her, and then disappeared as he proceeded through the hallway. Petra's mom went to Texas to visit her brother and learn about her family. While at her brother's house, she saw a picture of her father, and immediately froze. She recognized her father because he was the ghost wearing the hat she'd encountered at her home in East San Jose.

It is my belief that Petra's grandfather probably flew from Texas to California. I once read a report stating that ghosts can "fly at high speeds." Thomas Van Stein, an artist I met at Fort Tejon, suggested that ghosts can "fly up to 500 miles per hour."

QUIMBY ROAD

Ray A. is a security guard I met at Mountain Charlie's. Late one night, Ray and his friends got lost. While driving down Quimby Road, they noticed a man jogging on the side of the road.

Ray drove up to ask for directions, but the jogger ignored them. Instead, he disappeared right in front of Ray and his friends.

The ghost is a man who was struck by a vehicle and killed while he was jogging on Quimby Road. John Viray, a cook at Valley Medical Center, lived in the area and remembers the roadside memorial for this man, located where he died on Quimby Road.

Quimby Road. A jogging ghost haunts the road.

CAPITOL EXPRESSWAY, MILPITAS, AND VICINITY

Marianne Mai grew up near Capitol Expressway in East San Jose. Marianne's sister, Kathy, encountered several ghosts at her parents' house. After their father passed away, Kathy saw his ghost inside of his bedroom.

Late one evening, the ghost of their grandfather woke Kathy. The third time Kathy looked at the ghost of her grandfather, he disappeared.

Marianne's mother had a friend named Angie, and Linda was the name of Angie's daughter. Angie and Linda lived near Milpitas; and Mary Anne suggested that anorexia might have been the cause of Linda's death. While Kathy was in her parent's garage, she encountered the ghost of Linda.

Then Angie passed away and Kathy's brother is the one who found Angie's lifeless body on the couch. Kathy saw the ghost of Angie, also. Two months later, Kathy and Marianne's mom passed away.

PLEASANT ECHO DRIVE

John Viray's family used to live on Pleasant Echo Drive, in East San Jose. His parents used to babysit for his sister, Gerri, who never gave them any money for expenses, even though she earned a decent wage at the time. John's father spoke up one day, telling Gerri that she should be more considerate. She rebelled, and didn't come around for two weeks. Her father passed away before they'd resolved the issue.

It is the custom in John's family to pray for forty days after the death of a loved one. John was standing in the garage as family and friends were leaving their house on Pleasant Echo Drive. Gerri was approaching him when, all of a sudden, he felt as if a truck hit him.

John's face changed and resembled his father's face. When his sister looked at him, she did not see John, she saw her father. Gerri started crying and ran upstairs to her bedroom. A moment later, John looked and felt normal. They believe that their father's spirit used John's body to make contact with Gerri—to let her know that everything was forgiven.

At four o'clock in the morning, a light woke John's brother. When he sat up, the light moved along the ceiling, then disappeared. After John's family moved out of the house on Pleasant Echo Drive, John's father's spirit visited the daughter of the new owners. She was not afraid when she encountered him at night in the garage. She said that he was very nice to her and was glad her family purchased the house.

LONGVIEW DRIVE

Connie Ortiz and her family used to reside on Longview Drive, in East San Jose. For two years, things went haywire inside of the house, due to

Longview Drive.
The ghost of a boy haunts the house, which is a private residence.

the ghost of a boy who came out of the wall heater. Connie's ex-husband made contact with the ghost and he asked it, "What is going on?" The ghost of the boy explained to him that a gas stove had ignited and as a result, he'd died in a fire.

Connie's brother, John, did not have a pleasant encounter with this ghost. The ghost of the boy did not like John; so one day he chased John across the street to the neighbor's house. John's eyes were wide open.

While Connie was washing dishes, the sink caved in, water kept leaking, and they did not have much of an explanation as far as why the incident occurred. One day, Connie's children were watching the news, and their haunted house was one of the stories being covered by the news broadcast.

ALVENIA DRIVE

Gloria, Norma, and Connie Ortiz used to live on Alvenia Drive, in East San Jose. When they were eight years old, Gloria and her sister, Mona, both received matching dolls for Christmas. The dolls were tall with long blond hair. One night, Gloria and Mona woke up and were surprised to see the dolls moving around. They saw the eyes of the dolls moving, and frightened, they pulled their blankets over their own eyes. One day, Mona threw one of the dolls on to a bed and the legs kicked up in the air, arguably more than they normally should have.

Loyola Street

Norma lived on Loyola Street, in East San Jose. Her children told her about a particular room in her house having a ghost. Norma did not believe them until she spent the night in the room. Norma felt the ghost sit down on the bed she was laying in. She was unable to move or open her eyes. Norma prayed for the ghost to go away, and her prayer was effective.

Sometimes a ghost gets attacked. Norma's oldest daughter, Yvonne, threw a shoe at the ghost while it was standing in the room. The shoe did not phase the ghost.

The ghost of a man was sighted in the hallway; and they think it was trying to be helpful. One night, Yvonne was looking out the back window, and she saw the ghost of a man running fast around the backyard and looking at her. At first, Yvonne thought it was funny, but she got scared and closed the curtains. Lisa, Yvonne's sister, saw the ghost three times. The ghost was standing by the door and he was wearing a trench coat. The ghost appeared to be helpful because he seemed to be watching over Norma's kids; the ghost never entered any of their bedrooms.

King Norman's Toy Store and Chuck E. Cheese's

King Norman's Toy Store used to be located where Chuck E. Cheese's pizza parlor now exists on Tully Road. King Norman's was haunted by a girl who accidentally fell from the third level and died. Toys flew off of the shelves and a radio controlled car ran without someone controlling it.

Chuck E. Cheese took over the building and still occupies it today. Jason T. knew a girl who quit working at Chuck E. Cheese's after she saw the ghost of the girl on the second floor.

One of David Derr's students has a cousin who encountered the ghost of the girl while she was at the pizza parlor during the month of October, 2007. After seeing the ghost, the girl was crying and she insisted on leaving the property.

Lenny Salmon used to work at Chuck E. Cheese's, and after Lenny and a co-worker completely cleared a section of the restaurant, a table for six was set when they weren't looking.

The third level is the manager's office and I heard the ghost has been sighted up there. I focused on the third floor stairway when I took photographs of the pizza parlor. The orb was following me around the stairs and appeared in half of my pictures of the stairway. Several orbs appeared in one of the pictures I took.

Orbs at Chuck E. Cheese. The ghost of a girl haunts the third-level stairway.

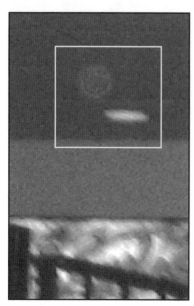

Detail of left orb.

MORE NEAR BERRYESSA ROAD

Ghosts have been known to imitate household noises and voices. Dianne Cruz lived in a haunted house near Berryessa Road, and has a sister named Jennifer. Evidently, a ghost was imitating her voice. Dianne and her niece, Kristine, were upstairs, and they *both* heard Kristine's mom, Jennifer, calling her from downstairs, but Jennifer was out of town. Dianne thinks the ghost may have followed her when she moved to the Rose Garden section of San Jose.

NEAR ALUM ROCK AVENUE

On New Year's Eve, 2003, we went over to Stacy and Ruben Chavez's house for a New Year's Eve party. Ruben's friend, Fernando, was a guest at the party. He told me about a haunted house he stayed in near Alum Rock Avenue. Fernando knew the house was

Detail of center orb at Chuck E. Cheese.

Detail of right orb at Chuck E. Cheese.

haunted, but he was not very scared to be there. Fernando saw the ghost of a boy who was wearing a striped shirt. Later on, Fernando found out the ghost of the boy not only lived inside of the house, he also died inside of the house.

The family's dog refused to go down into the basement of the house. One day, the dog was underneath Fernando's house, so Fernando went to get the dog out. He crawled underneath the house and he found his dog. The next thing he noticed was a spinning light moving around where he and the dog were. The spinning light scared the hell out of Fernando. He grabbed his dog by its hind legs and pulled the dog backwards, as he hurried out from underneath the house.

NEAR ALUM ROCK AVENUE AND WHITE ROAD

Bernadette Brasil was sleeping on the couch at her brother's house near Alum Rock Avenue and White Road. Somehow, the ghost of her grandfather had awakened her. Bernadette looked into the kitchen and noticed the ghost of her grandfather was sitting at the kitchen table. The ghost stood up, grabbed a glass out of the cupboard, filled it with water, then sat down and started drinking. After the third time Bernadette looked at the ghost, he disappeared. Bernadette yelled for her dad; and her dad explained to her that she had just seen the ghost of her grandfather.

ON THE EAST SIDE

Another story about Fernando getting scared took place in a house on the east side. He and two friends were renting a house. The day they were moving out, a mirror went flying across the room and smashed against a wall. Fernando and his friend's were petrified. All three of them ran out the front door. The ghost probably could have hit Fernando or one of his friends with the mirror—but this was not a violent ghost. The ghost was upset about them leaving because they will miss their company. A ghost may be more likely to feel lonely inside of a house that is vacant.

NEAR HIGHWAY 101 AND McKEE ROAD

Agnew's employee, Alan C., has a friend named Al R. who lived near Highway 101 and McKee Road. Al was in his late thirties when his mom passed away; and her ghost visited Al every night for one week. Al called Alan every night that week to tell Alan about his mom's ghost appearing.

Alan and Tim were over Al's house and the three of them were standing in the front yard. Nobody was inside the house, but Alan and Tim both noticed the kitchen window drapes close rapidly. They didn't say anything to Al, but they discussed the incident among themselves after they jumped into Alan's car and drove down the road.

JOSEPH D. GRANT RANCH AND BURLINGAME

I remember visiting Joseph D. Grant Ranch back in the early 1980s. At the time, there were horses still on the South East San Jose ranch, which is now a county park. In 1881, Adam Hubbard purchased the ranch which originally included 60,000 acres. Hubbard built the ranch house and J.D. Grant bought the property in 1927.

J.D. Grant liked the fact that near his sprawling acreage, James Lick was building the largest telescope in the world. One thing J.D. Grant had that William Randolph Hearst did not was a president for a guest. President Hoover stayed at the ranch after losing the election.

J.D. Grant had a son and two daughters named Josephine and Edith. Josephine Grant was the last person to live on the ranch until 1972, when she died in a car accident in Hollister. Edith Grant was mentally ill and had a daughter named Mimi who was in the custody of her sister and her husband.

Josephine and Edith disliked each other. They had fist fights in front of guests at the Grant's estate in San Francisco. Edith always started fights and also carried a gun. She shot and killed five people: three trespassers, a person in a bar room brawl in Livermore, and when Edith regained custody of Mimi because Josephine died, the fifth person Edith shot dead was her own daughter. Mimi was killed in Burlingame, and she might be haunting that property in Burlingame, if she is not at Grant Ranch where she had her own little house.

Ray Castillo is the first employee I met at Grant Ranch. A few years ago, Ray was the only person inside the cookhouse. It was after five pm, and Ray encountered the ghosts of two cowboys he nicknamed Slim and Shorty. Ray heard a voice about five feet away from him, and the voice asked, "Got a light?" Another voice replied, "Here you are." Ray saw two silhouettes standing in the cookhouse. One of the ghosts was slim while the other was short. Ray did not see the ghost smoking, but I explained to him that *some* ghosts do smoke tobacco.

I asked Ray if he had ever looked a ghost in the eyes. His answer was *yes*. There is the ghost of a boy who haunts the ranger station at Anderson Lake. Ray was face to face with the ghost before the ghost disappeared. The next time Ray sighted the ghost, the ghost was running around the ranger station. Two other men have also encountered the ghost. One of them was a ranger who transferred to a different park after he saw the ghost.

One day, Ray was inside of the ranch house, looking out the living room window. As Ray looked to the east, he noticed an orchard that existed years ago. He was seeing the past, which leads me to believe he is clairvoyant.

Ron Bricmont, county ranger, located some old pictures of the property which included the orchard. County Ranger, Ron, who worked

Orbs at the haunted Grant Ranch house.

at Grant Ranch since 1978, is an historical geographer. He is working on a book based on the history of Grant Ranch. And Ron contributed *all* of the information I have about the ranch, except for Ray's stories.

The Grant Ranch House is ideal for ghosts to reside because no one ever moved into the vacant house. The only people who enter the house are Ron and the weekend tour groups he brings through the house, along with some holiday event guests.

One of the apparitions that manifested inside of the house was the ghost of a woman. A deputy was walking by the living room window one evening, and when he aimed his flashlight at the house, he noticed the ghost and did not stick around.

In the early 1980s, the house was a ranger office, and the staff used to hear the sound of footsteps upstairs when no one was up there. The noise continued, and they went upstairs more than once to take a look around.

An employee was driving by the house at night, and he saw the ghost of a woman looking out of the upstairs window of Edith Grant's bedroom. During October 2005, Ron was giving a tour of the house, and Ashley was present. The tour group was inside of Edith's room, and Ashley was standing near the end of the bed. Ashley became convinced that someone invisible was inside Edith's room, and either wanted her to stay there, or the ghost wanted to follow her out of there.

Ashley quickly exited Edith's room, and will not go back inside of the room again. She might not even step foot in the house again. The ghost can literally keep Ashley inside of the bedroom by using a temporary-restraint method. The ghost could probably follow her home, too.

Employees have witnessed the lights flickering inside the house. Back in 2001, an employee was inside the living room, and he heard the sound of the front door opening and closing. This was followed by the sound of heavy footsteps in the entrance hallway. The employee, who was alone in the house at the time, immediately checked the entrance hallway. And he was surprised to see nobody there.

Between 1972 and 1974, some of Josephine Grant's employees were still working on the property. Between the front of the Grant house and the cookhouse is a brick patio. A number of people were situated on the patio and they heard loud noises coming from Joseph Grant's upstairs bedroom. The noise resembled the sound of furniture crashing into a wall. The group sitting on the patio assumed that someone must have sneaked inside the house, and was trashing Joseph's bedroom. The group of people quickly made their way inside the house and up the stairs. As soon as someone opened up Joseph's bedroom door, the noise suddenly ceased. They were surprised to find that no one was inside of the room, nor was anything broken or disturbed.

The group of employees decided to hold a séance to see if they could find some answers. The séance was *not* a good idea, and came to an abrupt end when the medium was trying to jump out of the second story window of Joseph Grant's bedroom.

An orb appeared in some of the pictures that guests took. I returned to investigate Grant Ranch a second time on July 28, 2007. I was a member of Ron's tour group, and I brought my Canon digital camera with me. An orb appeared in a picture I took of Josephine Grant's bedroom, downstairs. The orb in the picture is above a doorway. I took a *before and after* picture; the orb did not appear in the second picture I took. When the tour group went upstairs, I noticed a nice little area outside of the upstairs window. According to my photograph of orbs outside of the upstairs window, the ghosts moved to the outside of the house, probably because the tour group was upstairs at the time.

Before Edith Grant died, Ron met her one day when she stopped by the property and was accompanied by two nurses. Edith thought she was at one of her father's other ranches. And when Edith went into Josephine's room and recognized a picture of Josephine hanging on the wall, Edith said, "I don't like her."

FAMILY GHOSTS

My assistant ghost hunter, David Derr, teaches fifth grade. David used to have a student in his class named Isabel, and she has a twin sister. Both Isabel and her sister have the ability to see ghosts. At night, they've seen the ghost of their uncle, who told them, "Don't be scared."

Isabel's grandmother used to smoke cigarettes while hanging clothes to dry on the clothesline in the backyard. After her grandmother passed away, she noticed the laundry was mysteriously being folded.

What really alarmed Isabel was finding a burning cigarette near the laundry. The ghost of her grandmother was probably the person who was in the backyard smoking.

PICKFORD AVENUE

According to Dennis Hauck's book, *Haunted Places*, "The ghost of a woman dressed like a maid haunts the Gangelhoff House, which is a private residence on Pickford Avenue, in East San Jose. The ghost makes beds on the second floor of the house."(Hauck,1996,75).

The ghost is probably a maid who worked for the original owners of the Gangelhoff house, years ago. She makes beds because she thinks she is still alive and at work, or simply because she is a helpful ghost who doesn't like untidiness.

Chapter Two:
GHOSTS
OF DOWNTOWN SAN JOSE

STOCKTON AND LENZEN AVENUES

Susan Sablan used to live in a haunted house on Stockton Avenue. Susan's television exchanged information with her computer, and her television was not hooked up to her computer.

The lights inside of the house inexplicably went on and off, a pencil rolled across the table on its own, and there were cold spots.

At the intersection of Stockton and Lenzen Avenue was a train station, which no longer exists. The house Susan lived in might be built on top of an area where the railroad tracks once existed. Trains still use the track on Stockton Avenue, next to the H.P. Pavilion. Susan came to the conclusion that the *ghost* of a train was passing through her house.

Her friend came over to spend the night, and he was convinced that Susan was right. Other skeptics who came to Susan's house to spend the night were no longer skeptical about the ghost train, the following morning. At first the sounds of people walking around and strollers rolling were audible. Then the energy of the ghost train was felt, as it passed through the house.

The *only* other ghost train I know about is Abraham Lincoln's funeral train. Lincoln's funeral train "stops clocks and watches for eight minutes," according to Rosemary Ellen Guiley's book, *The Encyclopedia of Ghosts and Spirits* (Guiley, 1992, 223). Perhaps the ghosts who are affiliated with the annual event personally get off the funeral train to stop watches and clocks.

JULIAN STREET

In the late 1990s, Jerry Ruiz lived downtown at his father's house on Julian Street. Jerry's father's house was haunted by an old man, who previously owned the property and died inside the house. Jerry's father questioned the ghost, asking him, "Why are you inside my house?" The ghost of the old man answered, "This is *my house.*"

Jerry used to play rap music loudly, and the ghost used to turn down the volume. Sometimes, while Jerry was ironing clothes in the next room, he waited to hear the volume of the music being turned down in the other room.

When Jerry was young, he walked into his family's kitchen, and flying around the inside of the kitchen was the ghost of a witch on a broom. Jerry ran and told his parents about the witch, but when his parents went into the kitchen, the witch was gone. At the time, a television program was playing that showed a video of a witch in Mexico flying on a broom.

Jerry and his cousin have seen a ghost at the same time. The ghost appeared as a dark figure, standing in the middle of the street. There was a photograph taken of Jerry's family. In the picture was a television set (they never used) that was turned off at the time. A *short* ghost of a demon appeared in front of the television set.

Once upon a time, Jerry's father opened a restroom door and was surprised to see the short demon laughing. Jerry's father slammed the restroom door closed. When he opened it again, the demon was gone.

Ex-O'Connor Hospital security guard, Pam, told me a story about a picture of her family. The short ghost of a demon appeared in a picture of her family. The demon, "which resembled a warrior," was standing in a fireplace. There was no fire burning in the fireplace, at the time.

The Improv,
62 South Second Street

The Improv, located at 62 South Second Street, is a comedy club, that has a reputation among employees for being haunted. The building is one hundred and ten years old. There are unexplainable noises underneath

The Improv comedy club. Noises are heard behind the stage.

the stage and girls refuse to go down there. Orbs inside of the Improv have been captured on film. Also, the gate underneath the stage slams by itself.

ELEVENTH STREET

David Howard's father lived on Eleventh Street. Years ago, a farm existed on the property where the house now stands. Between three and three-thirty in the afternoon, people inside the house heard the sound of a car driving up the gravel driveway of the house. David's father got up and looked out the window, but there was no car there. David heard the sound of the gravel impacting as it would if a vehicle had just driven on it. Even guests have heard the sound of the phantom vehicle; they would ask, "Who just pulled up?" or "Who is here?" Every time anyone looked, there was no car pulling up into the driveway. The ex owner saw the ghost of an old man in the house on Eleventh and so did David Howard's father when he was in the garage of that house.

Sergio Perez and his wife used to sleep in a basement on Eleventh Street. Sergio's wife heard unexplainable noises, and she used a Ouija board by herself—which is not a good idea. Sergio was unaware that his wife had placed the Ouija board between the mattress and the boxspring of their bed. Ouija boards attract ghosts and some are not good.

Late one evening, the lights were off and Sergio heard the sound of *something* crawling up the wall. He also heard noise being made by cats in his neighborhood. Sergio was scared, so he prayed, and prayer is often effective when people are having a problem with a ghost. Sergio was unharmed by whatever was crawling up the wall of the basement. Most likely a demonic spirit was in his basement. (What was it? A feline shapeshifter? Who knows? It sounds like it was not like most ghosts.)

SOUTH TENTH STREET

County Nurse, Jackie G., introduced me to Benjamin, who lives downtown on South Tenth Street. For five years, Benjamin has lived at his residence on South Tenth Street, and he sees a ghost all the time. The ghost is a lady wearing a gown, and the ghost of the lady stares before disappearing.

The first time Benjamin encountered the ghost, he was scared to death. He ran through the back door, shut the door, locked it, then fetched some holy water.

Benjamin, another time, arrived home, and there she was in his driveway. He thinks the ghost has a smirk on her face, some of the time. Benjamin has sighted the ghost twice in one day, which is a *rare* occurrence.

An Asian lady used to live on the property. She moved out after seeing the ghost of the lady in the driveway. The first few times Benjamin saw the ghost at the back door, he was frightened. But he's used to the ghost now, and she has not done him any harm.

Another ghostly experience happed at 10:30 pm, and Benjamin was on Eighth Street and Margaret Ave. He was sitting down and talking to Jackie, a friend, when all of a sudden, a large shadow flew over him. The shadow alarmed Benjamin, as it flew toward Seventh Street, before vanishing.

FABER'S BIKE SHOP, 702 SOUTH FIRST STREET

Faber's Bike Shop at 702 South First Street, was in business for thirty years. Years ago, the newspaper featured a story about Faber's being haunted. I heard about bicycles pedaling by themselves.

I spoke with Alex Rivera, the owner of the shop. He did not have any stories about sightings, but Alex thinks the building is a "meeting place for ghosts." Years ago, a bar once occupied the building and more than one person died inside.

BUCKESTO PARK AND FRONTIER VILLAGE

James works for the city of San Jose, and one day, I met him at Buckesto Park. James lives down the street from the park, and his house is haunted. He has a water bed, and when a ghost sat down on his bed, he *really* noticed his bed moving. One time, James was unable to move or scream for a matter of seconds. He looked over at a crucifix hanging on his wall, and tried to stay calm while remaining mentally strong. When James was able to move and speak again, he stood up inside of the cold room and he told the ghost to show its self, but the ghost did not appear for him. James has a daughter and she sets up empty cans of *Pepsi*, so if the ghost comes by, he'll knock them over and she'll hear the warning.

James has a brother who worked at Frontier Village, years ago. One night, James' brother, getting off work at midnight, arrived home and saw someone in the front window. The chain lock on the front door was unlocked, and the front door opened up. He went into the house and saw his mom and thanked her for letting him in. His mom replied, "What are you talking about? I didn't open the door." The person he saw in the window was not his mom. It was a ghost who opened the door for him.

Another night at ten-thirty p.m., James heard the sound of someone knocking on the front door. He figured it was his girlfriend who was due home from work. When he opened the door, his girlfriend was pulling

H.P. Pavilion. The ghost of a girl haunts the pavilion.

up in her car, and there was no one standing at the door—at least nobody that he could see.

San Jose Arena

I worked at the San Jose Arena in the late 90s, which is now called the H.P. Pavilion, and the home of the San Jose Sharks. David Flores told me about the ghost of a girl being seen by security guards on the fourth floor, and other areas of the arena. I also heard a story about an employee seeing the ghost of a lady floating in the air, outside the arena window.

I went in to speak to the security guards there. The officer did not offer any information, but he mentioned reports of people seeing the ghosts of *animals* inside of the arena. When I asked him what kind of animals, he replied, "that depends on who you are speaking with."

I think I might remember this security guard, back when I was working there—and I'm lucky he told me anything, as he is very quiet about this kind of thing. Still, I believe he knows something! I know the circus has brought animals to the arena, but there is probably another explanation for the origin of the animal spirits—if in fact people have actually seen them at the arena. (They had a giant shark balloon that floated in the air!)

Faber's Bike Shop. A meeting place for ghosts.

NEAR MARTHA AND THIRD STREETS

Christina at Sun Micro Systems informed me of a haunted house near the corner of Martha and Third Street. Christina knew the lady who lived in the house with her husband and two children.

Unfortunately, the woman's husband went insane. He shot her and their two children. She ended up surviving, but her children did not. She was physically handicapped because her husband fired shots into her legs.

After she moved out of the house, her neighbors reported hearing the sound of children playing and balls bouncing. The neighbors had a grandchild who was around the same age as the two children killed. The neighbor's grandchild made contact with the ghosts of these two children. New tenants that moved into the house did not stay in the house very long.

JUVENILE HALL

Alexis Lindow told me about two inmates who died at Juvenile Hall, and I remember hearing about the tragedy years ago. The inmates wanted to escape from their cell, so they decided to start a fire next to the door. They were hoping the door would catch fire, but instead they both died from smoke inhalation. After the incident, inmates were no longer allowed to smoke cigarettes inside of Juvenile Hall. And presumably, another result of the incident was the existence of two ghosts. Supposedly, an entire wing is no longer in use because of so many problems and malfunctions.

An Agnew's employee, Frank, told me about Juvenile Hall being haunted, too. Frank's son spent the night there. He was alone in a cell and trying to sleep. He felt someone invisible grabbing onto his arm.

ALL AMIGOS ALANOS CLUB

All Amigos Alanos Club is located on North Almaden Avenue. I stopped by there and spoke with Anthony R., who told me the club has a ghost who slams doors. He didn't mention if there were any sightings of the ghost.

ST. CLAIRE HOTEL

The St. Claire Hotel at Market and San Carlos Street used to have a picture of the ghost of a woman walking in the lobby of the hotel. The ghost was wearing red shoes and the picture was so nice that an engineer at the hotel stole it and took it home with him.

Victor was working inside of the restaurant at the Hotel. He told me that every morning, a napkin on a particular table was moved and that a ghost is probably responsible for the activity occurring.

at The Hilton Hotel on Almaden Boulevard
operating on its own.

on North First Street, is notoriously
room #538. The ghost is a man
hat now, the television will turn
source (I was told this tidbit
ago), I seem to recall that the television came on by
same movie was always on the screen, and I think it was
cath Of A Salesman.

I interviewed some of the staff members, including two ladies at the check-in desk. A lady spent two weeks inside of the room hoping to make contact with the ghost. Her cell phone was acting strange. Another guest who came to see the ghost claims the ghost moved on and is no longer haunting room #538 at the Wyndham Hotel.

HAPPY HALLOW

The creek behind Happy Hallow is haunted by a ghost of a woman with long black hair, wearing a short red dress and a black belt. She is most likely a murder victim who's body was dumped near the creek.

Next to Happy Hallow is the Japanese Tea Garden and fish pond. Rod S., a police officer, had his patrol car parked in the parking lot next to the tea garden. It was late at night, and Rod was sitting in his car when suddenly a man appeared at his window. The man said, "Find my murderer."

Rod had *no* idea who this man was or what his problem was. The man continued to repeat his instruction, so Rod stepped out of his car to find out what going on. As soon as Rod noticed that the back of this man's head was blown off, he quickly stepped back into the car and stepped on the gas pedal. It's safe to assume Rod had a ghost encounter, and he feels nervous about his wife, Chrissie, bringing the kids to Happy Hallow.

I interviewed a couple of ladies who were working at Happy Hallow. They were not familiar with the ghost behind Happy Hallow, but they knew about the ghost sightings at the Kelley House, which is between the Japanese Tea Garden and Kelly Park. Located next to the ranger station is a house which is probably not the actual Kelley house, but the servant's quarters. The house is haunted by the ghost of a woman who has been sighted in the upstairs window of the house. An employee named Kelly C. saw the ghost, and so did two caretakers.

The creek behind Happy Hallow. A woman haunts the area.

The haunted Kelley House.

ANDY'S PET SHOP

Andy's Pet Shop, on the Alameda near Race Street, is haunted. And the ghost that haunts the shop is probably Andy, the ex-owner. The building was erected in 1929, and was a Department of Motor Vehicles building, a sheriff's office, and a post office.

Cassandra was cleaning the top of the dog kennels. She stepped onto a chair and started cleaning, when she noticed the ghost of a man walking by. She caught the top of his head, as he walked by and then disappeared.

One week later, Cassandra alone in the pet shop, was near the front window when she noticed the lights in back of the store clicked on. The lights were operated by a motion detector. Then a garbage can with wheels rolled out of the back room and into the hallway.

Sometimes, Cassandra hears one of the parrots saying *hello*, and wonders if the parrot is saying hello to Andy's ghost.

ST. JAMES PARK

Ray A's father, a county transit bus driver, encountered ghosts at St. James Park in downtown San Jose. At 9 am in the morning, he saw an Indian Chief at the park. At four a.m., he saw the pale ghost of an old man sitting on a downtown bench. When he looked again, the ghost was gone.

OLD COURTHOUSE, JULIANNE STREET

Terry V. suggested the old courthouse on Julian Street is haunted. Years ago, a lynch mob forced their way into the courthouse and hung a couple of men in St. James Park. The real question is: Do the two men who were lynched haunt the courthouse in misery, or do they haunt the St. James Park across the street from the courthouse because they were hung from a tree at St. James Park. Are there other souls about the building who were found guilty?

POST OFFICE, NORTH FIRST STREET

Dianne Cruz told me about the post office on North First Street having ghosts in the basement. The post office was built in 1893, and was originally located on Market and San Fernando Street. The post office moved to First Street, in 1934. I went there personally to "meet" the ghosts, but alas, no luck. Possibly the ghosts were former employees who worked there years ago—and they are now much too busy (still at work) for the likes of me.

EIGHTH AND WILLIAMS STREETS

Patty, an employee of Starbucks on Santa Clara Street, lives in a large Victorian house on Eighth and Williams Street. The house was once a convent which later became a frat house. The ghost of an old man wearing overalls haunts the property. Even Patty's roommate, a self proclaimed witch, was scared to be in the house when the power was out.

NEAR FIRST STREET

Maria Partida was living at her mom's house near First Street. For around two weeks, Maria woke up at night and found her son, Rolando, who was three at the time, in the kitchen. Rolando was underneath the kitchen table talking and playing with somebody invisible.

Maria's brother, who was also living at her mom's house, was looking in the mirror while combing his hair and saw the ghost of a young boy. When he turned around to look at him, the ghostly youngster would try to hide from him.

BACK FROM THE TRASH NINETEENTH AND JULIAN STREETS

My niece, Kiersten, has a friend named Tanya. She told me about her friend Jonathan's experience with a Ouija Board. Jonathan lives downtown on nineteenth and Julian Street. Jonathan asked the Ouija board, "How many people are inside of this room?"

"Four," said the Ouija board.

It was right. There were four people in the room.

But the board became unsettling. Jonathan *tried* to get rid of it by throwing it away. (People throw their Ouija boards away because they have suddenly become scared of them and they no longer trust the board's predictions—it might be giving them a negative vibe of paranoia and they're scared because they believe ghosts are actually interacting with them when they're using it.

But the board returned, and Jonathan found it back inside of his house.

Sheryl B's cousin in North San Jose threw her Ouija board away, and it came back, too. The ghost they were speaking to did not want to stop communicating. So the ghost pulled the Ouija board out of the garbage, hoping to be able to communicate with it once again. Ghosts will dumpster dive for them and bring them back into the person's room who originally trashed the board. Why? They want to keep communicating.

Tanya said to me, "You are supposed to say goodbye to the Ouija board, otherwise the ghost might get upset." I think a ghost might get upset with people simply being impolite.

ROLLERS AND BELLS

Priscilla Fuentes is a retired county employee. Her father remembers her hair rollers being pulled on by a ghost's hand at his house.

She also saw a spoon stirring around in a bowl on its own. It was Christmas time, and there were candy cane-shaped decorations with bells on them. Priscilla and at least one other witness observed the bells on the decorations jingling, and there was no natural explanation for the bells jingling without somebody shaking them.

EMPIRE STREET

Years ago, Henry Jacobo was riding a bicycle one night with a friend. They were passing Buckesto Park when they saw a man with a dog standing on the corner of thirteenth and Empire Street. Henry and his friend were unable to see the man's face because it was dark outside. They continued riding down the street, and they noticed the *same* man and dog they saw on thirteenth at the corner of seventeenth and Empire Streets. Henry and his friend were kind of tripping out, and when they saw the man and his dog again at the corner of twenty-first and Julian Street, they panicked and took off in a hurry.

Henry used to live in an apartment downtown and one evening, his roommate went out for a while with his girlfriend. While watching television, Henry noticed a ghost standing in the doorway, but he was not very scared.

SEVENTH AND ST. JOHN STREETS

When Henry was a kid, he and other kids in his neighborhood stayed away from a particular house on Seventh and St. John Streets. Their parents told them to stay away from this house because a witch supposedly lived there.

Troy Cattaveras and his family ended up moving into that house. Troy and his sister had experiences inside of the house which they never discussed with each other until they were both at a family get together, years later. They both remember seeing the same ghosts that appeared in that house.

When they were little, they would jump up and down on a bed. One time, the baby bottle fell off, bounced off the wall, and rolled underneath the bed. Troy's sister crawled off of the bed to retrieve the bottle. She came back up and told Troy not to go under the bed because there was a "monster" under there.

He did not listen to his sister. He went under the bed, but did not see anything but his bottle. He grabbed the bottle and when he came out from underneath the bed, Troy's sister saw a ghost coming out after him. The ghost looked like a person with *no* skin. Troy then saw the ghost and decided to challenge it. He went to grab it, but it suddenly disappeared.

Troy also encountered the ghost of a black angel. I asked Troy if it was a black person and he answered "no." The ghost was between five and six feet tall and was standing up with its feet inside of a grocery bag with eyes closed. One day, Troy's sister was in the kitchen, and she noticed there were two eyes on the floor, looking up at her.

It is interesting to note, too, that a witch used to live in Troy's house prior to his family.

WILLIAMS STREET PARK

Jean H. and Jerry R. told me about Williams Street Park being haunted by the ghost of a woman. My assistant and I have been to the park in the daytime, but we have not visited Williams Street Park at night to hunt for the ghost. So enter at your own risk.

QUANTUM, SYCAMORE DRIVE

I met Steve, a security guard, at Bernal Intermediate School. He was assigned to guard Quantum, which used to be located on Sycamore Drive where the city of Milpitas borders San Jose. Steve heard reports about fellow officers seeing a ghost while guarding Quantum's lobby.

The officers saw the ghost of an Indian on a horse come through the wall, stop and look at them, then continue on and disappear into another wall. The guards were frightened, and they ran out of the building.

Steve wanted to see the ghost, so he guarded the lobby himself, but he did not see the spirit of the Indian riding his ghostly horse. (Just how does a ghostly horse sound?)

For most of us, it is more than a challenge to try and see a ghost at a haunted place we're investigating, but those who go looking for ghosts are definitely increasing their chances of actually seeing one. The question is, will wanting to see a ghost and then seeing it, make you sorry you ever made the wish?

Chapter Three:
HAUNTED BARS AND EATERIES OF SAN JOSE

Downtown San Jose is the home of countless restaurants and bars that are reportedly haunted. Here are a few, but I'm sure that you will be able to find many more as you take your stroll through the haunted downtown area.

PATTY'S INN,
SOUTH MONTGOMERY STREET

Patty's Inn, Sports Bar—a chilling place.

Patty's Inn, on South Montgomery Street, is presumably haunted by the ghost of the original owner whose name was Patty. I spoke with Lisa M., and she told me about experiencing cold chills. At closing time, something will inexplicably fall, and she assumed Patty was responsible for the object falling. The beer coolers were kept closed, but they'd hear a popping sound resembling a cooler door opening and closing. The property was built in 1934, and Lisa said "the place is creepy, late at night."

Splash nightclub. More than one ghost haunts the building.

Splash Bar & Grill Waves Smokehouse, 65 Post Street

Splash Bar & Grill was formerly Waves Smokehouse. The building, located at 65 Post Street, was built in 1877 and is Historical Landmark #58.

The employee I spoke with at Splash was unaware of the haunting which took place inside of the building. Fortunately, I met Tone C. at The Hilton, who used to work at Waves Smokehouse, and he knew about the ghosts who haunt the property.

There are underground tunnels throughout the downtown area. Chinese smugglers used the tunnels during prohibition. A brothel once occupied the building at 65 Post Street. Tone C. told me about the small rooms he saw upstairs which were used by the prostitutes, which always adds to any ghostly historic story.

The ghost of a man probably resides in the basement of Waves. He was a bartender who worked there. The ghost had a habit of inappropriately touching women while they were down in the basement. The women would turn around and slap the co-worker standing behind them; then they had to explain to the manager why they'd slapped the co-worker with them. The co-worker got the blame and not the ghost!

Tone C. was in the upstairs kitchen cooking lunch for himself. The place was closed and it was daytime. Tone turned and noticed the ghost of a lady walking down the stairs. Tone went over and looked down the staircase, but the ghost of the lady wearing a dress had already disappeared.

Perhaps, she worked on the property when it was a brothel, years ago. The ghost of this lady scared the devil out of Tone C. When Tone mentioned the incident to Joel W., Joel was giggling, for he was aware of the ghost's existence.

Behind the stage at Splash is a cat walk. Tone noticed the cat walk was moving and a ghost was probably moving it.

GLO POLYESTERS,
FIRST AND SAN SALVADOR STREETS

Glo, formerly Polyesters, was a night club on the corner of First Street and San Salvador. Glo had a reputation for being haunted and it was the largest night club in downtown San Jose. I spoke with an employee at Angel's which is across the street from Glo. His friend was working as a bartender at Glo, before the club closed. The bartender was straightening bottles when he heard a bizarre noise that scared him. He did not like being there alone at night.

Maybe the ghost was affiliated with the club when it was Studio dance club, back in the 70s. Or perhaps the ghost is just monitoring the bartender's job performance.

PICASSOS,
SAN PEDRO SQUARE

Picassos, formerly Blakes, is located at San Pedro Square, in downtown San Jose. A bartender at Martini Brothers, named Chris, told me about Picassos being haunted. A waiter (named Chris) who no longer works at the restaurant had knowledge of the activity which occurred inside the restaurant.

I stopped into Picasso's for a drink, and Julio was bartending. He told me about his paranormal experience in the restaurant. It was 11:30 pm and Julio was the only person inside the restaurant. He was in the upstairs office when he heard a inexplicable tapping sound. The sound was loud, and Julio, wondering what in the world was going on, went downstairs. But the noise stopped. Nothing inside of the restaurant was disturbed. He heard the noise on at least two different occasions.

Could the tapping have been a ghost seeking attention or playing a prank? Or was it just a ghostly sound of the past being replayed by the atmosphere?

AGENDA,
SAN SALVADOR AND FIRST STREETS

Back in December 2004, I was a guest disc jockey at the Agenda night club on the corner of San Salvador and First Street. I spoke to the owner, and he claimed there are not any ghosts at the Agenda.

I said, "The basement is kind of creepy."

He replied, "Yes, especially when you are down there."

Picasso's restaurant—strange tapping.

Michael Ihdego, a friend of mine, was hired by the Agenda to be a disc jockey down in the basement. Michael was setting up his equipment, and he heard a noise behind him. He assumed it was Malcolm Robertson, his assistant. Michael was surprised to see Malcolm coming down the stairs because he thought Malcolm was behind him. As Malcolm descended, an invisible force pushed him and he almost tripped. A light moved closer by itself, and Michael speculates that the ghost was trying to help. Michael was scared and he moved to the upstairs patio where he was a disc jockey for a while.

MISSION ALE HOUSE, SANTA CLARA STREET

Chris at Martini Brothers used to work at The Mission Ale House on Santa Clara Street. The Mission Ale House has a reputation for being haunted, but I was unable to substantiate any ghost sightings. Chris is convinced that the basement of the ale house is haunted, however. He described the enormous basement where he heard disembodied voices, unexplainable sounds, and felt odd gusts of wind.

TRIALS PUB, 265 NORTH 1ST STREET

Trials Pub is located at 265 North First Street, in downtown San Jose. An employee at Teske's Germania Restaurant-Bar and Beer Garden told me about Trials Pub being haunted. The former owner, who moved to France, knew most of the ghost stories. I met with Rob, who's been the owner of Trials for a year and a half.

Rob heard a strange noise when he was the only person inside of the pub. Erin, an employee I spoke with, has experienced hot and cold spots, heard strange noises, and is afraid to be there alone.

I don't think Trials is a scary place, but it does have kind of a haunted look and sensation within the atmosphere. Another reason I believe in a ghost existing at Trials is because the local neighborhood ghost walk starts out at Trials Pub. Anyone frequenting a ghost walk assumes that first creepy starting spot has a story or two to tell... But not to worry—you're usually not alone on a tour...

EMMA'S EXPRESS, SANTA CLARA STREET

A lady who works at of Emma's Express on Santa Clara Street told me about seeing the ghost of her mother in the restaurant. Most likely, her mom's spirit followed her to work, or was stopping in to check up on her.

MIAMI BEACH CLUB, SAN PEDRO STREET

Miami Beach Club is located on San Pedro Street. I interviewed a security guard who works at the front door, and he told me about a guy who was stabbed and killed inside of the club. As a result, the club was closed for business, but they eventually reopened it. There is not a lot of paranormal activity occurring there, but things do move around here and there. No actual sightings were mentioned.

I tried to gain some information from employees working inside of the club, so I stopped in on a Thursday night. Unfortunately, no one had anything to say about the ghost. The first time I photographed the front of the club, no ghosts showed up on my camera screen. I returned a month later, however, to take more pictures. I turned my car around, stepped out to take two more pictures, and the orb appeared in my last picture. It is shown above the left hand side of the front door. I have several other pictures of the front door which show no trace of the orb.

The ghost probably knew I was there because of him, and he probably voluntarily posed for me and my camera. It was a nice and sunny day, but I was afraid to go back and try to make contact with the ghost. I *rarely* avoid an opportunity to confront a ghost.

TRES GRINGOS, SECOND STREET

Tres Gringos, on Second Street, is haunted by the ghost of a man wearing overalls and a cowboy hat. I interviewed Dave, who encountered the ghost of the man while he was down in the room that is located underneath the street. In front of Tres Gringos is a hatch

Mission Ale House. In the basement, disembodied voices are heard.

Trials Pub. Employees have witnessed ghost activity.

An orb above the left-hand corner of the door of Miami Beach Club.

Detail of orb above the left-hand corner of the door of Miami Beach Club.

on the sidewalk. This door is the entranceway to a room located down below the street. Weird noises have been heard by employees.

RED STAG LOUNGE, WEST SAN CARLOS STREET

The Red Stag Lounge, on West San Carlos Street, is haunted by the ghost of a little girl. Junior Ramirez manages the lounge on Sunday nights, and his mother has been a co-worker of mine for years.

Tres Gringos. A ghost was sighted in a room under the street. Highlighted is the hatch that leads down to that room.

Late one night, Junior was cleaning the bar and the ghost moved cups from table to table. The ghost also sings. Junior has heard her singing and so has the owner. Sometimes, Junior will hear the ghost talking in the daytime, and he tries to figure out what she is saying. Other times, Junior turns up the television or plays a song on the jukebox because he grows tired of hearing the ghost. He's also heard the sound of liquor bottles tapping together inside of a *locked* storage room. Junior unlocked the door and checked out the room, but there was no trace of the ghost, and nothing was disturbed.

MT. HAMILTON GRAND VIEW RESTAURANT, MT. HAMILTON ROAD

No restaurant in San Jose has a finer view than Mt. Hamilton Grand View Restaurant, on Mt. Hamilton Road, in East San Jose. Alex K. happens to know the chef at the restaurant and Lucy, the owner. Lucy sat at the bar with me and I told her about the rumors I heard including: the lights in the restaurant acting funny and the ghost of a girl being sighted on the outdoor patio of the restaurant.

Lucy knew nothing about the ghost of the girl existing, and has no idea who the ghost might be or where she came from. But she has heard "crazy noises" and has seen shadows inside of the restaurant.

Nobody died at the restaurant, which was built in 1954 by the owner of a bar that burned down across the street. Lucy acquired the property in 1960, and has been there since her late husband passed away.

The ghost of a singing girl haunts The Red Stag.

David Unger is Lucy's grandson and he made me a drink at the bar. Lucy said, "maybe the ghost of David's grandfather is here, keeping an eye on him." According to David, the restrooms are the most haunted area of the restaurant.

In 2005, David and a couple of friends were video taping the restaurant. They were standing behind a table near the front door. It was night time and they did not see the ghost that appeared on their video tape until they were replaying the video. A shadowy figure emerged from the restroom, walked by the wall, then disappeared into the dark corner. There was no way David or one of his friends could have cast the shadow that appeared because the three of them were standing behind a table on the other side of the room.

One night, it was after hours at the restaurant. David and a friend of his were playing guitar inside the dining room area. There were two chairs on the floor and only one light on inside of the restaurant. The kitchen door was propped open and David's friend noticed a shadowy figure standing in the doorway of the dark kitchen.

David looked over at the kitchen door and he saw the shadowy figure, also. The shadow was so still, and they assumed something in the restaurant was causing it and there was a natural explanation for the shadow. They ignored it and continued playing.

Ten minutes later, the shadow was gone, and suddenly there was a supernatural explanation for the shadow they observed. They both saw the ghost, who was walking through the kitchen, pass by the kitchen door. The next thing David and his friend did was exit out the front door of the restaurant.

I plan on returning to The Mt. Hamilton Grand View Restaurant for dinner, especially because the view is awesome. Maybe next time I visit I'll catch a glimpse of that shadow.

Chapter Four:
HAUNTED HOSPITALS AND CLINICS OF SAN JOSE

Hospitals all over the world are naturally haunted because people die there. Some souls remain and linger around a hospital for some time. Other ghosts include former employees who have passed away, but are still at work for one reason or another.

Valley Medical Center. Once in a while, an employee will see a ghost.

VALLEY MEDICAL CENTER

Valley Medical Center is a county hospital which was established in 1850. The hospital was originally located downtown on the corner of Market and Post Street. In 1871, the hospital was moved to 751 South Bascom Avenue, and opened up for business in 1875. The property on Bascom Avenue originally included a graveyard, which was turned into a parking lot in the 70s.

Susan V. was a supervisor who worked in the dietary department. After Susan passed away in the 90s, rumors of a ghost began to surface in the dietary department. Numerous employees claimed to have seen the ghost of Susan. Lenny S. noticed the ghost of Susan next to a hand-washing sink. David H. encountered her while he was exiting a walk-in refrigerator. David H. is under the impression that the ghost of Susan is monitoring progress, and is anxious to see him leave when he closes the department at night.

Ramon M. is an ex-employee, who used to hear the loud sound of the walk-in refrigerator door slamming, even though no one was in the area where it was located.

Chris S. heard the disembodied voice of a woman calling his name, and he has heard the voice humming.

John V. heard a woman's voice calling his name when he was in the kitchen.

Barbara M. heard a woman's voice say "hello" when she was the *only* employee inside of the department, at five a.m. Barbara M. and Alex K. both heard the sound of the department's entrance door closing. To their surprise, they did not see anybody when they walked over and looked to see who had just entered the department.

Rob K. was inside the department by himself and it was early in the morning. As Rob approached the tray line area, he heard music coming from an unexplainable source. Rob was the first person to tell me about some tacks, which hold up papers, falling out of a bulletin board near the ovens. David H. and Gloria C. both witnessed the tacks fall out and papers fly to the ground.

Employees heard the buzzing noise of an oven timer. That particular oven in question has not been used in over ten years.

Sergio P. found the door to the salad area refrigerator open after he personally closed it.

Joey S. was inside the milk refrigerator when the lights were turned off. He quickly exited the refrigerator to see who was playing a prank on him, but no employees were in that area. This happened to me, too. It was 5:45 am and I stepped out of the elevator on the second floor. I heard voices and I wondered who was in the cafeteria area so early in the morning. As I proceeded to walk towards the cafeteria, the voices stopped and there was nobody inside of the cafeteria.

Henry Jacobo used to be the graveyard housekeeper who was assigned to clean the dining section of the hospital's cafeteria. Henry's shift started at eleven am and ended at seven a.m. At three-thirty a.m., Henry heard the sound of a group of people talking. When he turned around to look behind him, the voices were suddenly silent. Henry also heard the sound of someone inside of the cafeteria conference room knocking on the door. Of course, there were no employees inside of the conference room so early in the morning.

I was standing near Abel's office, and I saw Emma D. and Abel H. standing in front of the elevator because someone was stuck inside of the elevator. Alex K. walked by the elevator and could actually see a trace of light coming from inside of the elevator, which meant it was stuck on the first floor. Abel and Emma heard a voice inside the elevator whistling and calling for their help. Sergio P. heard the person stuck inside the elevator ask for a glass of water. Finally, the voice was silent and the elevator door opened. After the door door opened, and Abel and Emma saw *nobody* standing inside, they looked at each other, then they quickly walked away.

The hospital morgue was temporarily located on the second floor where the old operating room was located. I went in to take a look at the morgue and I went unnoticed by staff members who were working in the area."

Henry Jacobo was walking on the second floor towards the main wing. Henry noticed an old man walk out of the morgue and continue down the hall towards the main wing. The old man was wearing scrubs and Henry saw him turning and walking down a hallway towards the central wing. Henry was walking behind the man, who must have been a ghost because when Henry looked around the corner towards the central wing, the man had disappeared into thin air.

I've heard the sound of drawers closing on their own inside of the cafeteria. In the restroom is a shower which has not been used by anyone in years. I noticed the position of the shower curtain was mysteriously changing for about two weeks. Sergio Perez was in the locker room and observed hangers moving around as if something invisible had brushed against them. He also heard a boom sound, and the light blew out.

Don P. has also heard noises coming from the shower area while he was using the restroom. Activity frequently happens inside of the department.

"One day David H. told me about windows closing on their own. I went downstairs to take a look; and as the two of us were watching a window, it slammed shut. Alex and I noticed an unplugged fan was slowly turning for a while."

It's no surprise that the basement of Valley Medical Center is haunted, especially because the hospital's morgue is located down in the basement. A housekeeper died of a heart attack while sitting on a bench that is located in front of the central supply department. Cathy Zitzer witnessed some of the paranormal activity taking place in the central supply department which is located across from the morgue, in the basement.

Cathy saw a book flying off of a shelf, and most likely, the book was thrown by a ghost. Johnny Johnson and Roman work inside of the central supply department. They have witnessed objects flying off of a storage shelf. According to Roman, "quite a few times, something unexplainably falls or moves." And they wonder who is in the back of the department. But when they've looked to see who was making the noise they'd heard, they did not see anybody.

Johnny and Roman heard someone in the basement crying for help. They ran out of their department and went looking around the basement to locate the source of the cry for assistance. They did not find anyone, and neither did the security guard who responded to help them search.

One morning, Johnny Johnson arrived early to work and decided to lay down on the couch inside of the property control building. There is an old piano stored on the second level of the same building. Even though Johnny was the only person there, he heard noise coming from the piano, and the only suspect, besides the ghost of the manager, was a bird who sneaks in.

Norman Canady works in a shop, inside of the hospital's basement. Norman and his brother were born with a caul, which is rare. People born with a caul (white membrane of amniotic fluid which covers the head of the newly born) are known to possess the gift of being able to see ghosts. Norman and his brother "weren't interested in having the gift and it went away."

Norman continues to see ghosts, occasionally. Out of the corner of his eye, he has seen them walk by the door of the shop and sometimes a ghost walks into the shop. Down the hall from Norman's department is a housekeeping supply storage area. There is a metal door which leads to a tunnel, and I went inside of the tunnel, years ago. Back in the 90s, the door to the tunnel shook late at night (a ghost?), and graveyard shift employees were scared of the door. They stayed away from it. The area is creepy—weird little noises.

Scott, who works at the clinic on Tully Road, worked at Valley Medical Center for eight years. During his graveyard shift inside of the mechanical room, Scott would often see someone walk by. Sometimes a ghost walked inside of the mechanical room; but when Scott looked towards the ghost, he did not see anyone standing there.

Louis G. works on the first floor. A man committed suicide in the restroom near the front entrance where 1st Central is located. I spoke with employees who observed a horrible mess of blood. According to Louis, when the patients are asleep at night, there are noises heard by the staff.

Bill Wulf was walking down the first floor hallway, and when he was passing the CAT scan room, he looked through the window and noticed a white silhouette of a figure standing inside of the CAT scan suite. It was late at night and Bill wanted to see who was inside the suite. He checked both rooms, but there was nobody inside of either room.

Adrianna told me about the old emergency room on the first floor being haunted. She knew employees who worked there.

Donnell T. had an employee named Sam. He was always complaining about seeing shadows late at night, while cleaning the second main area. The area was evacuated for several years, because of construction that took place.

Cathy Zitzer has heard the hand dryer blowing inside of the restroom. The hand dryer is motion activating, and these particular restrooms are locked, which meant there was nobody inside of the restroom who activated the dryer.

Norman C. told me about a particular room being haunted, inside of an Intensive Care unit. The television inside of room number 2 turned on and off by itself. The television's channels also changed, without explanation. And most of the patients who were put inside this particular room ended up dying. A doctor insisted that his patient was not put inside the room, so the staff put his patient into a different room.

Nina G. was assigned to clean the morgue and mop the floor. When Nina entered the morgue, she heard voices and thought to herself, "Good, there is someone else down here." When she went looking to see which employees were inside the morgue, she was surprised to see *nobody* was there.

Sergio Perez told me about a sighting that occurred on the third floor of the hospital. Sergio knows an employee named Gloria, and she works on the third floor. Gloria noticed a child was walking behind a couple of people, and the three of them were approaching a station where she was working. Gloria looked back down at her computer monitor's screen and continued typing on the keyboard. When the couple arrived at Gloria's station, she said to them, "I'm sorry. No children are allowed to be here at this time." The couple replied, "What are you talking about? We don't have any kids here with us." Gloria looked over the counter of the station, but did not see the child, who must have been a ghost that disappeared.

Norma O. and Denise P. were on break, and they were inside of a room on the fifth floor of the hospital's main wing. They noticed the shadow of a person passing by the door, and they wanted to know who it was. Cora was sitting at a desk nearby, so they opened the door and asked Cora, "Who just walked by?" Cora answered, " No one." They have seen the shadow passing by, on more than one occasion.

Silvia R. works on the seventh floor and not very many people go up there. Silvia hears noises coming from the vacant restrooms, located across the hallway from her office.

There are rumors that the hospital's mail room is haunted by the ghost of George. George is an ex-employee who passed away. On two different occasions, Henry's Pittsburgh Steelers hat flew off of a shelf and ten feet across the room. The hat landed on Manuel Barragan's lap, and he was frightened.

An employee, named Ruben A., used to work inside of the boiler room of the hospital. Ruben saw the ghost of a man inside the boiler room.

Nina G. knows some housekeepers who were in the old operating room on the second floor. They were working a graveyard shift, and one of the housekeepers noticed someone standing on the other side of a window. The housekeeper went back to confront the person, but the person vanished—they must have been a ghost.

Building W is the oldest building at Valley Medical Center. I heard stories about security guards being scared to go down into the basement of the building. The building was erected in 1912, and was the pest house used for patients with communicable diseases. The building then became the coroner's office, eventually became the human resource department, and is now the location of pharmacy administration.

Years ago, Denise Padia was assigned to clean the building. She heard doors closing on their own and the sound of banging coming from a heater. She decided not to stay, and she exited the building. A housekeeper, named Jessie, was cleaning the building when a chair rolled out into a hallway; Jessie was the only person inside of building W, at the time of the incident.

Jamie Clarke and Sheree Martin were in an office with the door open. They saw Leanne walking through the hallway, and there was a man following behind her. The man was a ghost who was no longer visible a moment later. When Jamie and Sheree walked out to the hallway, they saw only Leanne standing there. The ghost they saw was a bald white man wearing a green jacket. Herbie is the nickname they made up for the ghost.

The water turns on by itself inside the woman's restroom, and things have ended up missing. Doors close by themselves, and a shadow has been seen by employees inside Building W. An employee has a dog named Tequila, who acted very stressed when it was inside of Building W.

Jamie decided to hang up a Christmas stocking for Herbie the ghost. Herbie's stocking was hanging inside an office which is kept locked, and only two employees have the key to the lock. While the office was locked and vacant, Herbie's stocking was moved around. Also, the employees noticed the position of the stocking was periodically changing. Was he checking to see what gifts he might get? Or was he just moving the stocking around to show them a sign of existence? I'm inclined to think the latter.

Norman Canady worked at the Valley Health Building which is across the street from Valley Medical Center. On the third floor of the building was the OB/GYN Department. Most of the paranormal activity that Norman was aware of occurred inside of this department. Around midnight, doors closed on their own, lights went on and off, and at times, Norman was afraid to be there. He knows ex-employees who have seen ghosts inside the department.

On Saturday, November 16, 2007, Gloria Ortiz, Norma Ortiz, and Denise Padia were working overtime at Valley Medical Center. That afternoon, Gloria was working up on the sixth floor inside of the old cardiac catheter lab. She noticed a ghost walking by and the ghost was wearing blue jeans. Gloria was frightened and she insisted that Denise stay on the floor with her. The next day, Norma Ortiz was working on the fifth floor of the hospital's main wing. And she witnessed motion-activated doors opening on their own.

Another tidbit: A nurse at VMC did not believe in ghosts until her friend died and called her on the telephone.

Judy Coyle is a county employee who permitted me to use a story she authored, that appeared in the October 2006 Historical Society Newsletter.

> Pat Johnson was a nurse who worked at Valley Medical Center for twenty-nine years. She provided the story based on a professional group director, named Dorian Hostettler. Mr. Hostettler heard rumors about the old TB Ward being haunted. For years, rumors about the ward being haunted had circulated around the hospital. There were reports of furniture moving in the middle of the night, garbage cans being tipped over on a regular basis, and shuffling noises coming from the basement. Some employees were skeptical about the old TB Ward actually having a ghost. Mr. Hostettler decided to see for himself if the building was haunted.

> He spent the night alone inside of the building, and it did not take long for things to start happening. He witnessed a chair move into a hallway, and also heard noises he could not explain throughout the night. The following morning, Hostettler noticed furniture was moved around and garbage cans were tipped over. He was *not* interested in spending another night inside of the old TB Ward building again, which was eventually demolished.

> Some speculated that the building was haunted because it was located on top of an old Indian burial ground.

Some individuals get what they wish for when they are investigating a haunted place. They see a ghost or witness paranormal activity occurring.

Park Alameda Clinic

The Park Alameda Clinic is a county health facility, located on Lenzen Avenue. There are still traces of ashes on the ground of the basement because they used to cremate bodies there. Janitors who have been employed at the facility for a while have seen ghosts. I was told: "If I go to Lenzen clinic, I might even see a ghost." I didn't see a ghost when I visited the clinic on two separate occasions, but the place does have a haunted look and feel.

Ben was the first employee I met at the clinic. He took me to the pharmacy where Sylvia was working, and she contributed her share of

The Park Alameda Facility. A ghost was seen by an employee at the clinic and activity occurs in the basement.

information. Sylvia was on duty at the clinic one Saturday afternoon, and there was nobody else on the premises. Sylvia was inside of the warehouse and she was using the first-floor restroom. After Sylvia exited the restroom, she noticed the ghost of a little boy who was walking on the other side of a locked door. Sylvia heard the ghost's footsteps and she watched the ghost walk down the hallway.

Dave was working at the clinic when I went there in 2007. Dave has heard noises in the basement and he has witnessed chairs moving around on their own.

According to Art at Valley Medical Center, years ago the county jail was full and inmates were kept in the basement of The Park Alameda Clinic. One of the inmates was taking a shower and somehow a light fell from the ceiling, and he was electrocuted. The crematory is no longer used but because it is enormous, it remains in the basement until they figure out how to get rid of it.

Naturally, patients died at the clinic when it was a hospital and patients have died in clinics, too. Some of these patients might continue to linger on the property as ghosts. The ghost of the boy might have been a patient. He is probably responsible for at least some of the ghost activity occurring at the clinic. The electrocuted inmate could very well be an entity who's present at the clinic.

CHABOYA CLINIC

Most of the Chaboya Clinic was closed after the construction of the county's new clinic near the county fairgrounds on Tully Road. According to Scott at the Tully Road Clinic, there are quite a few stories about people seeing ghosts at the Chaboya Clinic, which was located on the corner of Tully Road and Mckee Road. Employees have seen doors open and close on their own, and toilets flushing by themselves. The clinic opened a new department and is operating.

EAST VALLEY CLINIC

East Valley Clinic is located in East San Jose. Dave at Park Alameda Clinic heard rumors about the clinic, including: lights not working, doors not opening, and ghosts of animals being seen on the property. There might be a pet cemetery located near the facility.

County security officer, Ross North, patrols East Valley Clinic, and he is unfamiliar with any reports of haunting that has occurred at the clinic. Ross did have a story about ghost activity he encountered during a shift he worked at the Tully Road Clinic.

TULLY ROAD CLINIC

Ross was assigned to patrol the clinic on Tully Road, which was built next to an Indian burial ground. It was 10:45 pm on a November evening when Ross began to hear strange noises. He was sitting at a station when he heard a sound that resembled the thick bottom of a glass tapping against a counter top. The sound was coming from the pharmacy, and Ross thought everybody had clocked out and went home for the night.

Ross looked at the security camera monitors and zoomed in on the parking lot, but did not see *any* cars parked in the lot. Next, he noticed motion-activated lights being activated, although there was no one inside the building. Ross heard voices speaking, and he went looking for the source of the disembodied conversation he was hearing.

Ross was thinking perhaps some employees were still inside the clinic. Ross was surprised to find absolutely nobody inside the clinic, and he decided it was time for him to leave the facility.

I interviewed Scott over the telephone, and since he started working at the clinic, he has to deal with some of the many things going haywire inside the clinic. An employee noticed a trash can opening by itself, and this was the type of garbage can that requires the weight of someone's foot to open the lid. Laser-activated sinks turn on and the water runs, but when you stand right next to the sink, the water shuts off. Batteries are having to be replaced at an alarming rate.

When I investigated the clinic, Tony was on duty, and he escorted me back to Scott's work area. Several employees contributed stories, including

Sightings and other ghost activity has occurred at the Tully Road Clinic.

the story based on the encounter Tony had with a ghost. Tony works in the pharmacy, and while he was using the restroom next to the pharmacy, he noticed the ghost of a boy in the restroom. A lady, who works at the clinic, saw the same ghost of the boy inside the women's restroom.

A ghost was seen walking out of the restroom by an employee. The employee tried to follow it but the ghost vanished.

Terrence has seen shadows around the clinic, in the late afternoon.

O'CONNOR HOSPITAL

Some of the hospitals I visited, including Regional Medical Center, are difficult to obtain stories about, especially if you are not speaking with the right employees at the right time. The only story I heard relating to Good Samaritan Hospital came from Roxy at O'Connor Hospital. She heard room number 124 had a ghostly presence. Three nurses observed a black shadow lingering inside of the room, and the patients inside the room were agitated because of the entity's presence.

Back in the 1800s, Myles O'Connor made a fortune in the mining business. Myles and his wife, Amanda, decided to build a sanitarium for the sick and the elderly. O'Connor Sanitarium was erected in 1889, and the facility was originally located on Meridian Avenue and West San Carlos Street.

I know the sanitarium was haunted because I have seen

**O'Connor Hospital.
Sometimes paranormal activity
occurs at the hospital.**

pictures of ghosts who have appeared in some of the pictures that were taken inside and outside of the sanitarium. There is a picture of the old sanitarium's nursery hanging on the wall at O'Connor Hospital. Among the two nurses and the newborn babies in the picture is a *transparent* lady wearing glasses and smiling.

After the hospital relocated to Forest Avenue in the 50s, the sanitarium on Meridian Avenue was demolished. A Sears Roebuck store was erected, and I remember being there when I was a child. Eventually, Sears was demolished. Today, Safeway and McDonalds occupy the space.

Registered nurse, Mary T., worked at O'Connor Hospital, until she passed away, back in the early 90s.

In 1997, a child and his mother were inside a room, on the third floor of the hospital's pediatric unit. A nurse entered the room, and they noticed the nurse was wearing an old-fashioned hat which nurses no longer wear. The nurse proceeded to tend to the child's IV. After she was finished, she exited the room. A while later, a different nurse entered the child's room to piggyback the child's IV. The patient's mother informed the nurse about the *other* nurse who had already piggybacked the boy's IV. The nurse was confused. So she went out to the nurse's station and asked her co-worker if she had any knowledge about the situation. She wanted to clarify if her co-worker was the other nurse who went inside of the patient's room. Her co-worker did not piggyback the patient's IV, and these were the only two nurses who were working in that section of the hospital.

Some wondered if the ghost of Mary T. had materialized and helped out the patient—especially because Mary worked on that particular floor, and wore a hat which fit the description of the hat the patient and his mother saw.

Mary Romesberg is an x-ray technician who works at the hospital. Back in 1997, Mary and a co-worker named Lennie were sitting inside the employee break room. The time was midnight, and the ghost of a lady wearing a yellow dress with blue flowers walked by the break room where they were sitting. The ghost of the lady walked past the break room and either continued walking through a wall, or simply vanished because the area leads to a dead end.

Mary did not want to react too soon. So before saying a word to Lennie, she looked at her to make sure she had also seen the ghost of the lady walk by. When Mary looked over at Lennie's face, she knew Lennie had also seen the ghost because Lennie's mouth was wide open.

I arrived to work at 4 pm and clocked in. I was walking on the first floor, and when I passed the director's office, I heard the sound of a door closing. I thought it was unusual for the boss to be at work on a Sunday, and I heard the noise of the door, a few hours later. The director was not at work that night, and there was no one inside her office. In the same hallway, there are motion-activated doors. I noticed the doors would be open even though no one was walking through the doors.

At three a.m., Eric G. was taking a body to the morgue. The doors automatically opened for him. One day, I stood and watched the doors because they were open. A hospital security guard joined me, and I asked him if he knew any ghost stories. During the entire conversation I had with the security guard, the doors kept opening and closing. The doors have since then acted normal without any problems.

Roxy R. was on the first floor, walking towards the visitors elevators. She was on her way back up to the second floor, and saw a man walk into one of the elevators. Roxy walked into the elevator, and as she was saying, "Push button number 2 for me," she realized the man whom she'd seen walk into the elevator was gone and must have been a ghost.

Roxy R. was working at the communications desk on the second floor. She noticed an old man wandering around the end of the second-floor unit, and that unit had been closed for five years. The old man was wearing a hospital gown and was probably a patient. Roxy immediately went down the hallway and said, "Excuse me sir, this section is closed right now." She reached the end of the hallway, but no longer saw the old man.

She searched every room on that floor, but never found the old man because he was a ghost who vanished, instead of sticking around to deal with her—and I don't blame him. Nurses have been scared to work in this section of the hospital, where the code blue alarm has been mysteriously activated, in the middle of the night. Code blue is an alarm which the staff responds to, when a patient with a serious condition needs immediate attention. The button to activate the code blue alarm is located at the nursing stations.

The heart health conference room is located at the beginning of the unit. Sheryl Washington used to lay down in there to rest, but she no longer does because she was having bad nightmares inside the room.

Between the two units is a room behind the communication reception desk. A Vietnamese nurse was resting on a couch inside of the room. When she awakened, she was unable to move or scream. She was barely able to move her head from side to side. This experience normally happens for a minute or less. Then everything returns to normal.

Near the operating room, an employee placed some carts against the wall and the carts were lined up in a row. When the employee returned a short while later, all of the carts were moved to the other side of the hallway.

A sterile processor saw a ghost while working near the operating room.

A housekeeper has seen shadows near the ambulatory surgery unit, which is in the old part of the hospital.

I was using a restroom down the hall from that section, on the second floor of the hospital. The time was 9 pm and I was getting ready to clock out. I was looking in the restroom mirror and all of a sudden, I heard some noise. I didn't know what the noise was, and I wondered if someone was coming down the hallway. I opened the restroom door, looked down the hallway, but I did not see anyone there. I turned around and looked inside of the restroom. I noticed the garbage can had a swinging metal lid that was creating the sound I heard. I did not touch that garbage can, which leads me to believe a ghost might be the one who pushed the garbage can lid, causing it to swing and make noise.

A man was on the third floor, visiting a patient at the hospital. As he was standing in front of the window at the end of the ward, he noticed the reflection of a man standing behind him. He turned around to look at the person, but the person was a ghost who had already disappeared. The visitor was a little shaken about the incident.

I was on duty at the hospital and I was walking down the hallway. As I was passing the communication reception desk, I heard the sound of something hit the ground. I looked around to see what happened and found a binder on the floor. There was no one sitting at the communications desk and there were no other employees working in the area. I came to the conclusion that a ghost had probably pushed the binder off of the communication reception desk in order to get my attention.

The time was after 4 pm and the fire alarm was activated. I glanced out the hospital window and noticed a fire truck was parked in front of the hospital. A security guard I used to know, by the name of Pam, was on duty that afternoon. According to Pam, how the fire alarm was activated that day remains a mystery.

Lan is an employee who works in the hospital's CAT scan suite. Lan noticed the light inside of the CAT scan room was acting funny for a few minutes. Even though there was nobody touching the control switch on the wall, the light became brighter for a few seconds. (Lan's apartment is haunted, too, and Lan was sleeping on the couch because she was scared to be inside of her bedroom. Lan's friend was over her apartment and she saw the ghost of a woman sweeping inside of Lan's apartment.)

Lan was walking down a hallway with a co-worker of hers. As they were walking, Lan's co-worker felt something hit her. She and Lan both turned around to see what it was that hit her. There were no other people in the hallway. And when they looked on the ground, they found a penny which was most likely *thrown* by a ghost.

Graveyard shift employees experience the most activity. Hospital beds and other equipment have unexplainably moved around. Hospital beds were seen changing position without assistance. The engineering department received a letter from the company who manufactures the beds. They claim a bed moving on its own is probably just a mechanical error taking place. Employees heard a disembodied scream coming from a room inside of one of the intensive care units.

The staff approached the room and found there was nobody inside. A priest was called in to perform an exorcism. Lan was walking down the hall, and a co-worker in the hallway asked Lan if she was going upstairs for the ceremony. Lan ended up following the co-worker upstairs. They entered a second-floor nursing unit, and inside the unit was a small group of employees and a priest. The priest asked the group to write down on a piece of paper any negative feelings they were experiencing at the moment. Everybody wrote something down, then the papers were collected and burned. Next, they picked a stone and came up with a positive feeling to write on the stone. (I don't know much about the exorcism as far as why the priest had people writing things down. I do think the exorcism was a success. I have not heard any reports of haunting since the group gathered and I walk through that intensive care unit five days a week and have not noticed anything unusual happening.)

When Jose Diaz started working at the hospital, back in 1998, a housekeeper by the name of Edelmira told Jose, "Be careful! There is the ghost of an old lady in a wheel chair wearing a big hat." On the first-floor hallway, there is a picture of a lady who fits the ghost's description. The lady is a nun sitting in a wheelchair and she is wearing a tall hat.

Edelmira encountered the ghost of the lady while she was down in the hospital's basement. The restroom in the basement is arguably haunted. A door in the basement leads to two separate restrooms. On numerous occasions, I was using one of the restrooms and I heard someone open the entrance door, then go into the other restroom and use it. I did not hear the person leave, and when I opened up the door, I was surprised to see the other restroom vacant with the light off and the door open.

Philip is an ex-employee who noticed the entrance door closing when nobody was inside of the restrooms. While I was using the restroom, I heard the sound of a person's footsteps coming down the hallway. They opened the door and they checked to see if the door to the restroom I was inside was locked. I saw the door handle jiggling. They went into the restroom on the other side, and I never heard them leave. A minute later, I was leaving the restroom. And I expected to see the door to the other restroom closed because I was convinced there was someone in there. When I opened the door, I once again saw a vacant restroom with the door open and the light off. The only time I became scared while using that restroom is when the light outside of the restroom turned off by itself. The light was on when I entered the restroom, and I was expecting the light to still be on when I exited the restroom. The light was off, and darkness tends to make a situation a bit scary.

Greg Woods was resting in a room inside of the hospital's basement. When Greg woke up, he was unable to move his body for a matter of seconds. This is what happens when a ghost sits on top of a person, or when a ghost is holding a person down. First of all, Greg focused on moving his foot. Then he slowly was able to move the rest of his body until everything was back to normal a minute later.

Bernie was standing near the guest elevators and he was watching a couple of ladies who play music at the hospital, once in a while. One lady plays a harp and the other plays a keyboard. A few minutes after Bernie stood there enjoying the performance of the two musicians, he felt an invisible hand on his shoulder.

Jose Diaz was working inside of the Wound Care Clinic, on the second floor of the hospital. Early in the morning, Jose heard someone screaming, but the scream was unexplainable because no one was in the area. Jose's mom passed away that evening. The next time Jose heard something unusual, he heard a strange moaning sound. On that night, Jose's sister-in-law's mom died. The story reminds me of a harbinger of death. A screaming banshee is a harbinger of death, forewarning and announcing someone's death, shortly before it occurs.

Marie P. and at least one other employee were sitting in the diet office. A box moved off the top of a file cabinet and landed on the floor of the diet office. They assume a ghost pushed the box off the cabinet.

A nurse by the name of Marie was working on the fifth floor. Out of the corner of her eye, Marie observed the silhouette of a ghost, standing in the doorway of a room.

Ramon C. was inside a room on the fifth floor. And there he noticed the silhouette of a ghost with long hair. The ghost was ducking behind a bed. Ramon went to look for it, but he did not see it again.

Valentine Granado was taking a break in the old section of the hospital. Valentine was standing in front of a window at the end of a hallway, on the fourth floor. As he was looking out the window, he saw the reflection of the ghost of a man standing next to him. Valentine turned and looked around for the ghost, but he did not see it again.

The fourth floor of the old building has a reputation for being haunted. I was conversing with an employee at a sporting goods store. Even he was aware of the haunting rumors about the fourth floor in the old building. His mom was a nurse at the hospital.

Flo is an employee at the Cardinal Lounge, and she used to work on the fifth floor at O'Connor Hospital. Flo told me a about an incident that occurred on the fourth floor. A nurse working on the floor noticed a Rabbi walking in the hallway. The Rabbi walked past her and went into a patient's room. The nurse noticed that the Rabbi did not come out of the room. The Rabbi must have been a ghost because the nurse went into the room looking for him, but there was no trace of him to be found.

AGNEWS STATE MENTAL HOSPITAL

Agnews State Mental Hospital originated in Santa Clara, back in the 1800s. A second facility was erected in the 50s, and that facility is located on Tasman Drive, in North San Jose. Agnews in Santa Clara was closed, and Sun Micro Systems now occupies the property where the hospital stood. There are more ghosts at Agnews in Santa Clara than there are at Agnews in San Jose.

Frank was an employee at Agnews, and he had a co-worker by the name of Carlos. Carlos was walking in the basement of Agnews and he suddenly noticed the ghost of a lady, coming through the wall and disappearing into the other wall on the other side of the hallway. Carlos was definitely frightened by the apparition.

Jose Diaz was working inside of the basement at Agnews. At two a.m., all the patients were sleeping and the place was supposed to be quiet. But Jose heard organ music playing and the source of the organ music remained a mystery.

Jose was assigned to clean the inside of the administration building. He looked at pictures of the hospital that were hanging on a wall. Some of the patients who died at the asylum appeared as ghosts in some of the pictures. Employees were able to recognize deceased patients that posed for the photographs.

Chelsea A. at Century 25 Theatre heard ghost stories about Agnews, including reports of organ music being heard by employees.

I visited the peaceful grounds of the facility and went inside of the kitchen to see if any employees had a ghost story to share with me. The employees working inside of the kitchen were unaware of any ghosts in the kitchen.

Jennifer was standing in front of a building—she worked in an office on the second floor—so I approached her and asked if she knew any ghost stories about Agnews. Jennifer has worked at Agnews for two years and sometimes she becomes scared while on duty. Around eight p.m., she's heard noises including the sound of people running down the hall. Sometimes Jennifer blasts the music on her radio so she does not have to tolerate hearing the strange noises coming from outside her office door.

A lady I met at Buckesto Park by the name of Chris; she works for the City of San Jose. She had a friend named Debra, and Debra's car horn did not work. Debra had not rested much for a couple of days and she was extremely tired while driving her VW on Highway 880. Debra accidentally fell asleep at the wheel and her car was heading toward the center divider.

She would have ended up in a bad accident, but her broken car horn was *somehow* beeping; she awakened in time to steer her car away from the center divider. Unfortunately, Debra was involved in a tragic car accident anyway. The top of Debra's scalp was hanging off, and she was dead. Fortunately, Debra was brought back to life and she remained in a coma for one month.

Agnews Hospital. Employees have witnessed ghost activity.

The doctors assumed that Debra was brain dead, but she was not. She did end up paralyzed as a result of the accident. When Debra was in a coma for the month, she saw and spoke with the ghost of a young girl. One day, the ghost of the girl was going through the tunnel to the other side. Debra asked the ghost of the girl if she was going to go along with her through the tunnel.

The ghost answered, "It's not your time yet." When Debra recovered from being in a coma, she asked the hospital staff where the young girl was, and Debra knew the girl's name. The staff members were shocked because the girl Debra met had died in a fire, years ago when her family's house burned down. The house used to be located where the hospital was erected. After the incident took place, the staff members were scared of going inside of Debra's hospital room.

O'Connor Hospital employee, Brian Glenn, used to work at a convalescent home that was located on the border of San Jose and Los Gatos. The hospital was located on Bascom Avenue, and there was a patient at the hospital named Freddy Kramer. Freddy was a nice guy and Brian got along well with Freddy. However, there was a mean nurse working at the hospital, and her last name was Dawson. Nurse Dawson was tall and served in world war two as a nurse. She was known to put a washcloth into a patient's mouth if she had trouble keeping the patient quiet during a bath or a procedure.

Freddy despised Nurse Dawson, and when Freddy passed away, his ghost was chasing Nurse Dawson down a hall. Nurse Dawson was more terrified than ever. She ran as fast as she could and she hid inside of a medication room for an hour. Brian Glenn knew something was wrong. He went into Freddy's room and he saw the curtains moving around on their own. And the room smelled like incense.

Chapter 5:
250 GOLD RIFLES

THE PLIGHT OF SARAH

In 1839, Sarah Winchester was born in New Haven, Connecticut. Sarah married William Winchester in 1882, and Sarah gave birth to a daughter who died less than two months after she was born. William Winchester died in 1881, and an occultist told Sarah that the spirits who were killed by the rifle William invented were responsible for the deaths of William and her daughter. And if she did not buy a home and continue building more rooms, she was going to die next.

With a fortune of nearly twenty million dollars, Sarah moved to California in 1884. Sarah purchased an eight-room house from a doctor, and construction on the estate continued nonstop for thirty-eight years.

There are different theories based on why Sarah built a mansion with so many rooms inside of it. Los Gatos historian, Bill Wulf, thought Sarah's house was the result of "architectural amusement." Maybe Sarah thought she could hide from the spirits who were after her. She slept in different rooms throughout the mansion, and her servants were given a room number so they knew what room she was staying in.

I personally believe Sarah was accommodating some of the spirits who were killed by the rifle that her husband invented. Others think she was crazy and that's why there is a stairway leading to a dead end. Maybe the dead-end staircase was to confuse the spirits who were after her. Maybe the spirits wanted her to build the staircase. They were capable of coming through the ceiling to walk down the stairs. Perhaps either Sarah or the spirits were trying to teach us that ghosts can pass through the ceilings and walls of the mansion.

Sarah was an intelligent lady who conserved water and was very productive. Sarah sold a lot of fruit, was listed in phone books as a fruit grower, and developed a process which quickly dried the fruit from her orchards.

If Indian spirits were residing at the Winchester mansion, they didn't have to share the house with Sarah for six years because Sarah foolishly believed the world was going to be flooded. She moved into a houseboat and did not move back into the mansion until six years later; that story reminds me of Noah's Ark.

The Winchester Mansion.

At least three ghosts haunt the property—Sarah and two of her employees.

INSTRUCTIONS FROM BEYOND

Sarah held séance's between midnight and 2 am and supposedly received building instructions from spirits who attended her séances. Sarah used a communication device similar to a Ouija board, and with automatic writing, she received written messages from spirits. It sounds as if there actually were good and bad spirits at the Winchester mansion.

An author by the name of Allen V. doubts the Indian spirits killed by the Winchester rifle actually followed Sarah Winchester to California. While many ghosts do appear at the scene of their death, there are ghosts who have been sighted in different states than the ones they died in. For example, from the earlier story, Petra's grandfather died in Texas, but was seen here in California. Al Capone died in Florida and his banjo playing continues to be heard at Alcatraz. Furthermore, he "appears next to his grave in Hillside, Illinois" (Hauck, 1986, 160). Ghosts can bi-locate, and have followed people out of places here in California.

According to Antoinette May, who spent the night inside the mansion with Sylvia Brown, Sarah "discovered a black hand print on the wall of her wine cellar, and the spirits told Sarah that a demon was responsible for the hand print" (May, 1977, 53). I have personally heard of demons leaving hand prints—even on one's person.

The *Guinness Book of World Records* listed The Winchester Mystery House as the longest continuous building project. (Construction at Valley Medical Center might not occur twenty four hours a day, but the ongoing construction of the hospital has definitely outlasted the thirty eight- year construction period at the Winchester Mystery House.) Sarah was clearly obsessed with the number 13. I think the reason she was obsessed with this number was because she felt unlucky. Even though she inherited a fortune, her husband and only child were dead, and she was convinced there were angry spirits that wanted to kill her. These were truly unlucky circumstances, indeed.

I attended several of the flashlight tours which are conducted at the Winchester Mystery House on Friday the 13th. Employees have heard the sound of hammers pounding. A man who maintains the property and cleans the windows told me that when he is working alone at the house early in the morning, he hears strange noises. He said to me, "The question is not: *Is* the house haunted? The question is: Are you scared to stay the night alone inside of the house?"

THE DAISY BEDROOM AND OTHER HAUNTED AREAS

The first time I ever heard the term "ghost quake" was when I interviewed Eric, who was working inside the gift shop. Eric told me a story about two authors who felt the floor shaking while they were spending the night in the Daisy Bedroom. Some people believe the shaking was the ghost of the 1906 earthquake. (I've heard about a school classroom in the Philippines where shaking mysteriously occurred.)

Richard Winer and Nancy Osborn co-authored a book titled *Haunted Houses.* The two authors spent the night in the Daisy Bedroom. Nancy heard a broken piano being played, and they both felt the floor shaking, although there were no reports of any seismic activity that occurred in the area. They also heard the sound of footsteps outside of the Daisy Bedroom. There was no one else inside the mansion at the time (Winer & Osborn, 1980, 33-49).

Eric told me a story about an employee by the name of Allen Weitzel. In 1980, Allen locked up the gift shop and he walked back into the storeroom. When Allen returned to the gift shop, he found the door leading to the courtyard was unlocked.

One year later, Allen turned off all of the lights inside of the mansion and locked the place up. He walked out to the parking lot, and the lights inside the house were still off. After crossing the street, Allen noticed the lights on the third floor of the vacant mansion were turned on. Allen also found water spilled on his desk, paperwork, chair, and office floor. On his desk was a pencil holder that was full of water. Most likely, Allen was the victim of a ghostly prank.

Back in 1955, Arlene Bischel was temporarily blinded while she was walking through the Winchester Mystery House. After Arlene exited the mansion, she regained her eyesight.

According to a news article written by Bill Stroble, an employee by the name of Brent Miller heard breathing and footsteps near the room where Sarah Winchester died. He was awakened by the sound of someone working with a screwdriver. Brent had a friend by the name of Gary Parks who captured a ghost on film while he was taking pictures at the Mystery House. The ghost is of a man wearing coveralls (Stroble, 1981, *San Jose News*).

According to Alvin Guthertz, in 1975, a psychic investigator by the name of Jeanne Borgen was in Sarah Winchester's bedroom conducting a midnight séance. All of a sudden, it looked as if Jeanne was turning into an old lady. She was in pain, was unable to walk, and she screamed for help. A short while later, Jeanne was back to normal and stated that she was "overpowered by a gentle ghost" (Guthertz, 1976, 52-55).

In 1980, an office manager by the name of Sue Sales saw a ghost sitting at a table. The ghost was presumably Sarah Winchester. Jack Stubbert and his son, John, went into the house to paint. It was early in the morning, and John saw the ghost of a man wearing white coveralls. The ghost walked up a flight of stairs, then vanished.

A marketing clerk by the name of Allison Paker saw the reflection of a ghost walking across a room inside of the mansion.

Devon Grover was a tour guide who saw the ghost of a man in the basement. The ghost was wearing white coveralls and was pushing what was probably a cart. Two additional tour guides saw the same ghost while they were down in the basement of the mansion.

On one of the numerous occasions I visited the Winchester Mystery House, Patrick was the tour guide. Patrick heard his name being called more than once when he'd arrived to work early in the morning; he was the only person inside

of the house. Patrick has smelled the scent of chicken noodle soup while he was in one of the kitchens. Chicken noodle soup was Sarah Winchester's favorite.

Michael Suite told me about someone seeing the ghost of a man at the mystery house. The ghost was pointing to an undiscovered room that was boarded up.

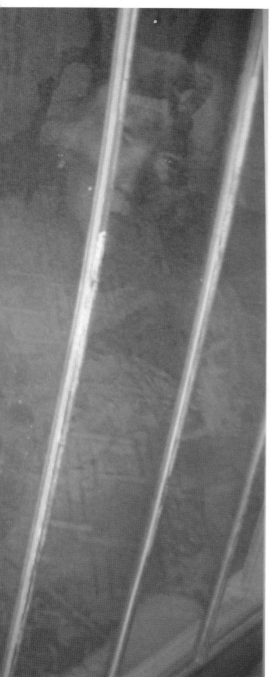

David Derr was watching a television program that was filmed at the mystery house. The camera crew was inside of the mansion, and a camera happened to be aimed at a window. Caught on film was the ghost of a man walking in the garden. The ghost passed by the window and he was probably one of Sarah's employees.

Pounding noises have been heard at the Winchester Mystery House. I met an employee by the name of Jennifer T. and she was inside the mansion during the month of October 2007. Jennifer was the only employee who was standing near the séance room and she heard a loud knocking sound. An employee found a shattered light bulb inside the séance room.

OFFICIALLY HAUNTED

The Winchester Mystery House is one of two properties in California that has been declared officially haunted by the Chamber of Commerce.

I met Anthony Rodriguez at The All Amigos Alanos Club. Anthony used to work at the Mystery House and he saw the ghost of Sarah Winchester looking out of an upstairs window. Anthony was in the backyard area

Presumably the ghost of Sarah Winchester. *Courtesy of Greg Woods.*

and he immediately ran into the house to make sure that no one was playing a prank on him. Anthony knows other employees who have seen the ghost of Sarah Winchester looking out of a window.

The Ghost Trackers organization ran an ad in a local paper, announcing a meeting that was going to be held at The City Lights

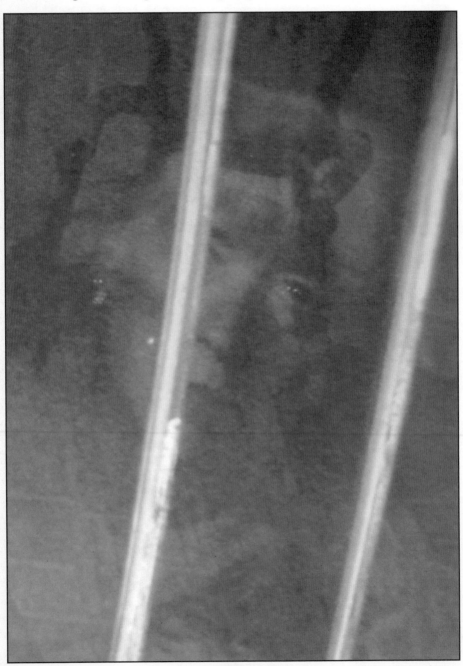

Detail of previous picture. *Courtesy of Greg Woods.*

Café in Santa Clara. On the Saturday morning of January 25, 2003, David Derr and I arrived at The City Lights Café at eleven a.m. Alas, circumstances prevented that meeting from taking place, but I decided it was an opportunity for me to take charge of the discussion. There were four people waiting, so I rounded up a lady by the name of Nancy B. and three other women who were school teachers. The six of us gathered in the back room of the café, and I attempted to show them (with illustrations) that a ghost consists of energy and so forth. I asked if any of them had ever seen a ghost.

Nancy has not seen a ghost, but she claimed that the ghost of Sarah Winchester established contact with her while she was using a Ouija Board. This event took place in Los Gatos back in the early 70s, and someone on the premises was related to Sarah Winchester. The communication between Nancy and Sarah lasted for several months.

Sarah said, "Her daughter died, and she died screaming of a heart attack." One night, Nancy was communicating with Sarah, but it was late and Nancy was tired. She wanted to go home, but the Ouija Board told her, "You'll die in a car accident." After reading that message, Nancy stayed put for a while. I don't know if Nancy was actually going to end up dead if she had immediately went to her car and drove home. However, I do think it was possible, especially if a ghost causes someone to have an automobile accident.

Another time Nancy was communicating with Sarah, and Nancy asked Sarah if she would appear. Sarah replied, "You will get scared to death." People *have* been scared to death as a result of seeing a ghost. Seeing a ghost can cause a person to become so frightened, they die of a heart attack. When I saw a ghost, I was too scared to look at the ghost a second time.

Sarah Winchester also told Nancy that she has "250 gold rifles hidden inside of a chimney." My eyes were wide open after hearing Nancy mention the gold rifles. Finally, the day came when the communication between Sarah and Nancy came to an end.

Sarah was financially capable of affording that many gold rifles. So the next day, I visited The Winchester Mystery House to see if I could find out any information indicating that the gold rifles might actually exist. There are forty-seven fireplaces inside The Winchester Mystery House. If there are in fact 250 gold rifles hidden inside a chimney, finding the rifles would compare to finding a needle in a haystack. I went into the Winchester rifle museum to see if there were any rifles that came from a batch of 250. Inside the museum is a nice gold-plated rifle which was one of *250* rifles that were given to the 250 members of the Winchester Rifle Association. The Winchester Mystery house is at 525 South Winchester Boulevard.

A MYSTERY TOUR

During the month of July 2007, O'Connor Hospital employees, Greg Woods and Julie Maciel, were on a tour of The Winchester Mystery House. Greg was taking pictures with his digital camera. The ghost of an elderly woman, who I assume was the ghost of Sarah Winchester, appeared in one of Greg's photographs. I think Sarah liked Greg, and that was the reason she was standing next to Greg. Either Sarah was accidentally photographed by Greg, or she volunteered to have her picture taken. Her image was reflected off the window of a closed room.

Greg's picture just might end up on the Mystery House web site. Regardless, check the site out at www.winchestermysteryhouse.com to learn more about this mysterious house.

Chapter Six:
HAUNTED SCHOOLS OF SAN JOSE

Schools all around the world are haunted, and I have never heard of a child being harmed by a ghost while they were attending school.

INDEPENDENCE HIGH SCHOOL

Independence High School is located on Jackson Avenue in East San Jose. The school theatre is haunted by a ghost named George. When I visited the theatre at 3 pm on a sunny day, it was quite dark and kind of creepy inside the theatre's lobby. I walked into the theatre and started taking pictures.

When I reached the stage, Pam Melvin and a couple of her students were on the stage. Pam was a pleasure to interview and she was very informative. George was not killed at the theatre, so Pam is unsure about where the ghost of George came from and why he haunts the theatre at the school. No one knows how old George was. Pam and others know he is a friendly but sometimes annoying prankster. The last time there was paranormal activity occurring at the theatre was during the summer of 2007.

People are frightened when they experience the ghost of George for the first time. Pam is used to George's presence, however, and does not fear him. Some students refuse to be inside of the theatre by themselves.

The ghost of George hates having to listen to the music of Michael Jackson, except for *Thriller*. While the compact disc player is playing, George pushes the forward button so the next song on the disk starts playing.

Strange Light Switches and Meetings

A dance teacher was using the theatre for a meeting. There are four different light switches inside of the theatre. One switch is on the back wall, two switches are on stage, and one switch is in the control booth where George has been known to hang out.

Pam has not seen George's face or clothes, but his silhouette has been sighted moving around inside of the control booth while nobody was inside of the control booth. The lights inside of the theatre kept turning off, though the door of the control booth requires a code and a key. The control booth has an alarm which will become activated if anybody breaks into the control booth.

Independence High School Theatre.

Presumably George's orb at the top of the picture.

While standing on the stage, the dance teacher could see there was no one standing near any of the four light switches. Somehow, the lights were turned off and she had to turn them back on more than once. The ghost of George was probably inside of the locked control booth, and he was probably the one who was turning the lights off.

George has never interfered with a show that was taking place at the Independence High School Theatre.

Pam asks her students if they've said good morning to the ghost of George. During class presentations, she has noticed a seat in the down position which leads her to believe that the invisible entity of George attends certain meetings. When the meeting is over, the seat that George was sitting in springs back up into position because the seat is no longer being held down by the weight of this interested ghost.

An ex-teacher was skeptical about the ghost of George actually existing. The teacher was directing a play with another teacher. He happened to bring his pet German Shepard inside the theatre that night. The German Shepard went to the fifth row and began growling at an empty seat and did not stop growling until the ghost took off.

A Shy George

The ghost of George is more active when people are not around. Pam has an office which is located behind the stage and she props her office door open with a full one-gallon can of paint. Pam finds the paint can moved, and her office door shuts when nobody else is inside the theatre. Moving the can of paint is one of George's pranks.

Students become scared when they sense the presence of George standing behind them. Once in a while, the theatre is vandalized; Pam wishes George was willing to scare off the hoodlums who vandalize the theatre.

She used to work in a building that was downtown on Second Street. Formerly a brothel, a stage company occupied the building when Pam worked there. She encountered multiple ghosts inside of that building, too.

HAUNTED SCHOOLS
NEAR DOWNTOWN

NOTRE DAME HIGH SCHOOL

Notre Dame High School is on Second Street in Downtown San Jose. The school is reportedly haunted by the ghost of a pregnant nun who hung herself from a balcony. According to the Shadowlands haunted directory, the gym is no longer in use because of the haunt.

I visited the nearly spotless campus of Notre Dame High School to try to validate the reports, and spoke with a groundskeeper who knows about the ghost of the pregnant nun. According to him, the gym is still in use. He insisted that I call Mary Beth, the school's principal—even though speaking with a school principal has never been my favorite thing to do! I tried calling her twice and my phone bill is the proof of my attempt. The only voice that came on the line was the voice of an answering machine which unsuccessfully directed my calls and failed to connect me with a member of the staff. Phew!

BURNETTE ACADEMY

Burnette Academy is located north of Notre Dame High, on Second Street. After basketball games, cheerleaders have heard the sound of someone falling near a stairwell that is located next to the locker room. Years ago, a girl was running up a staircase which leads to an upstairs classroom. She accidentally tripped, fell, and died because of her injury. The ghostly sound of the girl's fatal accident is heard at night time.

EAST SAN JOSE

ARBUCKLE ELEMENTARY SCHOOL

Arbuckle is an Elementary School located near King and Story Roads. A boy was murdered at the school back in the late 70s. The boy was repeatedly stabbed in the back, and supposedly, the ghost appears for some of the people who pass by the school in the evening.

Also, people have reportedly seen a knife sticking out of the ghost's back. Can't be good...

DOVE HILL ELEMENTARY SCHOOL

Dove Hill Elementary School is located next to Highway 101 in South San Jose. Reports exist about a ghost that haunts the school's basketball courts in the night time. People know the ghost's name because he happens to be wearing a name tag. People don't know the ghost by face because they cannot see it.

Michael T. is the name of the ghost, and he has been sighted by teachers who work at the school. A teacher approached the ghost of Michael to ask him why he was there so late at night. She took off running after noticing that he did not have a face.

I think Michael has control over his face appearing and he is not interested in showing it to those who encounter him on the basketball courts.

At Dove Hill Elementary.
A ghost by the name of Michael haunts the basketball courts at night.

While at the school at night, some students have witnessed lights inside vacant classrooms turning on and off on their own.

Oddly, there is no record of anyone dying at Dove Hill Elementary.

SILVER CREEK HIGH SCHOOL

According to a report received by the *Shadowlands* web site, the ghost of Amy hung herself inside of the Silver Creek High School theatre.

I went to the high school to investigate the report about Amy. A school employee claimed he has never heard about the ghost or the supposed suicide taking place, and neither has his mom who taught for years at the school.

One guy told me, "If the theatre does not have a ghost, it should have one." I agree with him because it definitely has a creepy appearance.

PIEDMONT HILLS HIGH SCHOOL

Piedmont Hills High School is on Piedmont Road in East San Jose. The high school is reportedly haunted by the ghost of a distraught girl who hung herself because her parents died in a car accident. The ghost has been sighted in the school's hallways and has been known to open and close doors at the school.

SLONAKER SCHOOL

Slonaker is located near King Road. The sounds of children playing while the schoolyard is vacant have been heard, and the ghost of a child who was accidentally run over by a car haunts the school.

CHAVEZ ELEMENTARY SCHOOL

A particular classroom at Chavez Elementary School is haunted. Hazel H. is the name of the teacher who wanted a different classroom because the one she was teaching inside of is haunted by a ghost.

There have been no sightings of the ghost, but the ghost has made its presence known. Hazel was the only one inside her classroom, and she heard a noise coming from the back of the room. The sound of papers shuffling could be heard, and she figured a mouse was causing the noise. She stood up and walked to the back of the classroom to see what was going on, but all of a sudden the noise stopped.

Hazel walked back to her desk, sat down, and the noise started again. Then her desk moved a foot and a half by itself. Hazel was scared and she ran out of the classroom.

The next story David D. told me was about the spelling cards that were pinned on the wall inside of Hazel's classroom. The cards were turned as if the ghost was trying to spell a word with them.

The last report I heard was about a pencil sharpener inside of the classroom that was seen turning by itself.

YERBA BUENA HIGH SCHOOL

Yerba Buena High School is located behind Kelley Park on Lucretia Avenue. Behind the school are horse stables which were reported to be haunted by the ghost of a man who used to own the property. The stables are between Kelley Park and the high school.

I paid the stables a visit and met Heida who has lived on the property for twenty years. She had no knowledge about the stables being haunted, but she lived in a house on the property, and was told by the builder's son that the house was haunted. The house was torn down a while ago, though.

BERNAL INTERMEDIATE SCHOOL

According to a short book written by Michael Boulland, Bernal Intermediate School near Santa Theresa Boulevard is "haunted by the ghost of a beautiful young Spanish woman. A janitor encountered the ghost on the second floor of the school. An elevator at the school that required a key was operating with no one inside of it, and a bottle of paint unexplainably exploded inside of an art classroom closet" (Boulland, 1996, 23,24,31).

Bernal Intermediate School is haunted by the ghost of an Indian girl.

Steve is a security guard I met at Bernal. He has not seen a ghost at the school, but the students tell him about the ghost.

Interestingly, David D. and I explored the 2,000-year-old Indian burial mound which is next to the school's playground. Could there be a connection? One never knows, but it's worth thinking about...

OVERFELT HIGH SCHOOL

Overfelt High School is located on Cunningham Avenue near King Road. It's on the *Shadowlands* list because "a janitor who was killed back in the 1980s haunts the high school at night."

I met a kid who attended Overfelt, and he told me about a student's leg having scratches on it after the student got out of the swimming pool. The scratches resembled claw marks. I was told that a student had drowned in the swimming pool.

DEL MAR HIGH SCHOOL

Del Mar High School is the most recent addition to the *Shadowlands* list of haunted places. "In 1942, a boy was murdered by his best friend near the Del Mar High School football field. Witnesses have reportedly seen the ghost of the boy running down the bleachers." According to the Shadowlands directory, "Screaming can be heard if you go to the football field approximately at 3:15 a.m."

EVERGREEN COMMUNITY COLLEGE

Evergreen Community College is on the *Shadowlands* list because the school is reportedly "haunted by the ghost of a girl who hung herself in the middle of the campus. The ghost was seen by some of the students who have attended night classes at the Evergreen Community College.

SAN JOSE STATE

Established in 1870, San Jose State University is haunted for numerous reasons. When I arrived at the campus to gather information, the first person I met was a security guard by the name of Ferdinand. He informed me about building YUH being haunted by the ghosts of Japanese detainees who were detained there during World War Two.

YUH

YUH is an old gymnasium that is used for various sports. When people walk by the gymnasium at night, they sometimes hear ghostly voices and cries emerging from the inside of the vacant gym.

Students were playing volleyball inside YUH the first time I went inside to investigate the gym. The basketball team was practicing the next time I explored it. As I walked around the gymnasium, I didn't feel

World War Two detainees haunt the YUH building at San Jose State University.

The University's pool was closed because of an unexplainable drowning.

any weird vibes. Furthermore, the inside of the gym does not have a scary appearance.

Maybe the ghosts at YUH are not into sports these days...

The Indoor Pool

The creepiest area that I noticed at San Jose State University was the indoor pool which is located right next to YUH. Ferdinand mentioned this indoor pool, and according to him, a student was practicing in the pool and ended up drowning.

After several other students drowned in the pool, the circumstances were questionable and the pool area was closed for good.

Because the pool area is located right next to YUH, I wonder if the ghosts residing at YUH were displacing their aggression and drowning students who were swimming in the pool.

I was only able to stand at the locked gates of the area and take pictures. As I stood at one of the gates, I heard some kind of brief noise emerging from the vacant pool area. A ghost?

Dorm Rooms and Halls

The next person I met was Devika. She is the campus tour guide at San Jose State University. Devika told me about a female student who died in a dormitory room which is located in a section of the campus called the Bricks. The telephone inside of the room where the girl died unexplainably rings for no reason.

Yoshita Hall is rumored to be haunted along with Hoover Hall and Royce Hall. There are rumors of a student dying during an initiation. There is a red plank on top of Tower Hall and supposedly, a student fell to his death while walking on the plank, which is high above the ground.

Alexis Lindow told me she was walking around the university in the daytime. While she was walking, she heard the footsteps of someone walking behind her. She turned around to see who it was, but there was no one behind her.

Chapter Seven:
Ghostly Encounters in West San Jose

Century 23

A ghost appeared in a projector room at Century 23 Theatre.

Four of The Century Theatres are on Winchester Boulevard, and three of them are located next to the Winchester Mystery House. The employees I met at Century 21 movie theatre did not provide any information about the theatre being haunted. An employee at Century 22 was told about a ghost being sighted in the A house section of the theatre. The employee did not know if the story was true or false. The two employees working at the front door of Century 22 knew about Century 23 being haunted.

In the late 90s, employees were telling me stories about items being shuffled around, including cups inside of the storeroom. During the month of October 2007, I returned to the theatres for an update on paranormal activity.

Gabe was working when I arrived at the theatre that evening. According to him, an employee by the name of Dave saw the ghost of an old lady in the projector booth. Dave was startled by the incident.

CENTURY 24

Less than one mile south of Century Theatres 21-23 is Century 24. Back in 1994, I worked at Century 24, and I never personally saw any ghosts or experienced any unusual activity. Not so, with other workers there.

Nevin was one of my assistant managers at the theatre. When I saw him at the Almaden Twin Theatre, he told me, "Century 24 has a ghost." A guy who cleaned the theatre late at night witnessed the ghost of a lady walking down an isle inside of the theatre.

HAUNTING NEAR WINCHESTER BOULEVARD'S TOYS'R'US

Next door to Century 24 movie theatre on Winchester Boulevard is Toys "R" Us. Al Mai used to work there, and the activity he encountered took place in an upstairs storeroom. Al heard dolls talking and other strange noises.

One time, Al was riding a pallet jack as if he were on a skateboard. He was rolling along, when all of a sudden, he felt as if he had run into an invisible brick wall. Al never did find the reason for the jack suddenly stopping while he was on it.

Nearby Residences

Al's mom's house is not far from the store. Al was eating lunch at her place and he heard a sound behind him which resembled a person crunching a jaw breaker. His mom was sitting across the table, but she did not hear the noise. Had Al brought a ghostly companion home for lunch?

Across the street from Toys "R" Us on Winchester Boulevard is Magliocco Drive. (We were watching *Unsolved Mysteries* at Kammy Miller's place on Magliocco Drive, and that episode motivated me to eventually hunt for ghosts aboard *The Queen Mary*.)

David Howard lives near Magliocco Drive, and at his residence, a bottle of water was being thumped by an invisible finger. A cap flew off of a bottle of soda pop, as well. They think a ghost of a girl is haunting the place. David and his wife heard music and thought it was coming from outside, but the music was coming from a clock radio in their bedroom, which turned on by itself. David saw his bed go down, too, as if a ghost sat down on it.

STARBUCKS

Less than two miles south of Toys "R" Us on Winchester Boulevard is the Starbucks coffee house. Starbucks might have a ghost because a man was fatally shot in front of the store. The employees at the shop are not positive that the place is haunted but they encounter little, but dramatic, situations, which are not a big deal to them. Still, small incidents make them think...

CENTURY 25

Located by itself in the West Gate Shopping Mall is Century 25 movie theatre. The theatre is definitely haunted and a lot of activity has taken place inside. There is a rumor about a lady who was the original owner or manager of the theatre. Supposedly, she hung herself inside of the projector booth.

Inside the women's restroom is a particular stall which is the center of activity for the bathroom. When ladies open the door to use the toilet, the door slams back in their faces. It sounds to me as if a woman died inside of that stall.

Other incidents involve Alexis and Trevor Lindow, who are married and working at the theatre. Trevor was the only person inside of the projection booth. He was starting a movie, when a ghost threw a wrench at him. Fortunately, the wrench missed Trevor and hit the side of the projector.

Alexis and Trevor were inside the projector booth and Trevor went downstairs for a moment. Alexis was sitting on a pillow and suddenly, it was so cold, she could see her breath. The next thing she noticed was a door opening and closing by itself. Alexis was scared and she exited the projection booth. Talking and singing have also been heard emerging from the projection booth area. Near the lady's restroom, employees have also heard a women's voice humming a tune.

They have also heard growling noises coming from behind the screen. Once in a while, a homeless person sneaks behind the screen to go to sleep for the night and the employees will have to kick them out of the theatre. When growling noises are heard and they don't find a vagabond sleeping behind the screen, it is surmised that the sounds are being made by a ghost.

Barry B. told me about an employee by the name of Matt Ryan who works at Century 21. Matt was visiting Century 25 one evening and he noticed the ghost of a woman walking through the theatre's lobby. The ghost walked out the front door and disappeared into the parking lot area.

It was the first day on the job for Alexis and she had not yet heard about the theatre being haunted. As she was putting seats up inside of the theatre, some of the seats were moved back down, and that requires the weight of somebody sitting down in the chair.

Chelsea A. was cleaning the theatre and she noticed a ghost moving in a chair. The ghost of a woman has been observed sitting in a seat and waiting for the film to start. After the projector starts rolling the film, the ghost stands up, walks down an isle, then disappears from sight.

Trevor and the others brought me inside of the theatre after a film was over and the crowd was gone. They showed me the seat where the ghost of the lady sits, and they also showed me a cup that is resting on the ceiling of the theatre. The ceiling is so high, I don't know if there is a ladder that tall. (Maybe there's a ladder on the back of a fire truck that might reach that high up.) I'm as curious as anybody about how the cup is being suspended. Is the cup glued to the wooden beam next to the ceiling of the theatre? Is there a thumb tack holding the cup in place? Did a ghost in fact fly the cup up to the ceiling, and there is a paranormal explanation for the cup not falling down? No one knows how the cup made its way to the ceiling, or how long the cup has been up there. Sometimes, ex-employees from the 70s stop by to visit Century 25 theatre. And these people know all about the ghostly occurrences and they know about the cup on the ceiling of the theatre.

Alexis Lindow once spoke with the ghost of a young girl inside of an elevator. The ghost of the girl did not dematerialize in front of Alexis. The ghost walked off the elevator and Alexis had no idea the girl was a ghost until she noticed a picture of the girl hanging on a wall. Alexis inquired about the girl and was told the girl was dead. Alexis gave me the notion that the ghost of the girl is in pretty good shape, emotionally; considering she had been raped and murdered.

The employees also told me about a room underneath Century 25 that none of the staff has ever entered. They think they've found a locked entrance door which leads to the room below the theatre. A mystery to be sure, and one wonders if the ghosts have a place to hide...

If someone wants to see the ghost that haunts the Century 25, I recommend watching a film on one of the two screens inside the theatre. The screen on the left hand side is where most of the haunting takes place.

There are no reports of anyone being harmed by the ghost while inside of Century 25, but you could get a good scare!

El Paseo Area

El Paseo Shopping Center

Across the street from Century 25 is the El Paseo Shopping Center. Inside the shopping center is the AMC Saratoga Sixteen movie theatre complex. This complex is on the *Shadowlands* list of haunted places because it is reportedly "haunted by a ghost that has been sighted inside of projection booth number 5. Theatre number 5 is where most of the paranormal activity takes place. Muffled laughter and voices have been heard inside of the complex."

I visited the complex to see if I could find more about the theatre haunts, but the employees I spoke with knew nothing about it. So what or who is behind the haunting at projection booth number 5? Has the ghost chosen a select few to interact with and left the rest in the darkness of the theater? Is there a reason why not everyone knows the story? Maybe a trip to AMC is in order—just keep your eye on projection booth 5...

FRUITDALE AVENUE NEAR SOUTHWEST EXPRESSWAY

Alexis Lindow used to live near the intersection of Fruitdale Avenue and Southwest Expressway. The houses in that area have thick wooden doors because families with a psychotic member resided there. If the psychotic family member flipped out, the families remained safe in rooms behind the thick wooden doors.

Alexis told me a chilling story about one of the families that used to live in the house she eventually moved into on this street. A man started flipping out and his wife locked the thick wooden door so he was unable to cause any harm to her.

The problem was, he extensively harmed himself. He was dying to see his wife. And he cut himself into pieces, attempting to make his body smaller so it could fit underneath the kitchen door. He ended up bleeding to death.

Alexis first encountered his ghost walking by her bedroom door. At first, he said a word or two as he passed her bedroom while walking down the hallway. Then he started entering Alexis's bedroom and the conversation between them accelerated. Sometimes, the ghost would not let her sleep, but she never mentioned a word about him being mean or harming her. Alexis was unable to see the ghost's legs—I'm not positive, but this could be due to the fact that he severed his own legs.

A significant fraction of all ghost sightings include cases in which witnesses are unable to see the bottom half of a ghost's body. I was surprised when Alexis said, "the ghost was not covered in blood." She was able to see the face of the ghost and he used to hide inside of her closet. Sometimes, Alexis opened her closet door and noticed the ghost standing behind the clothes that were hanging.

I would be frantic if I knew a ghost was hiding inside of my closet—blood or not.

VALLEY FAIR SHOPPING CENTER

David Derr used to work at a vitamin shop inside the Valley Fair Mall which is now the Westfield Shopping Mall on Steven's Creek Boulevard. I went in to visit David, and he thinks a ghost either followed me into the shop, or was already there. Ten minutes after I departed, David witnessed several bottles of *Zia* natural makeup, one by one, falling down and rolling off a shelf—without reason or cause.

THE GHOST OF AN IN LAW

Fely E. retired from O'Connor Hospital and she lives with her husband Harold. I knew Harold because he retired from Valley Medical Center. One evening, Fely was in her living room and she noticed the curtains were moving. There was a unusual gust of wind inside of her living room and Fely knew there was a ghost present.

Fely said to the ghost, "If you are here for a peaceful visit, that is all right. But if you are here to scare me, then you get the hell out of here." I always thought Fely was a tough lady, considering her age and size.

Fely looked out of the living room window and she saw the ghost of a man standing on the lawn near the sidewalk. She did not recognize the spirit until a few days later. Harold's brother died and Fely had never met him. At the funeral, Fely recognized Harold's brother because he was the ghost who had visited her, several days before his funeral took place.

GUITAR SHOWCASE

On December 24, 2006, I was inside of the Guitar Showcase swap shop on Bascom Avenue. The swap shop is located across from the main store, and the building houses used equipment that is sold on consignment.

**The Guitar Showcase shop is haunted by a former employee.
Ghost activity is minimal.**

I have been inside many music stores over the years, but not like this one. That day before Christmas, something happened which I have never experienced before. A guitar fell off of the wall by itself. I was standing in the drum section, when all of a sudden, I heard the sound of an electric guitar banging against the floor of the store.

A guy on duty at the store walked over to the guitar that was now on the ground. He said to the customer he was assisting, "I guess we have a ghost."

This was the only time I ever personally experienced anything unusual happening at the swap shop, which used to be a recording studio where a big name or two recorded. Lately, I was purchasing some equipment from the store and I inquired about the place having a ghost. The answer was yes.

Dave was the first employee with whom I conversed. He mentioned doors opening and closing on their own and guitars swinging. Bert told me that the ghost might be Dan—a guy who used to be a manager at the store and he'd passed away.

The two fanciest guitars for sale used to hang next to the sales counter. The guitars would swing back and forth, and there was no other explanation for it besides...it was being done by a ghost. There have been no reported sightings of the ghost of Dan, though.

Another employee claimed he's always thought the property was haunted ever since his dad brought him there when he was a kid.

THE GHOST OF AN INDIAN NEAR ALMA & WILLOW STREETS

Steve is a fellow I met through a friend, back in the nineties. Once in a while, he'd stop by my work, and tell me a ghost story which took place at his mom's house. Steve's mom lives near Alma and Willow Streets.

In 1985, Steve and a friend of his were at Steve's mom's house. A ball of light had come between them and they could not see each other for a moment. They heard voices coming from this ball of light which soon disappeared from their sight.

Steve and his nephew heard a radio playing inside his nephew's bedroom. They went into the bedroom to take a look, and they noticed the radio was unplugged and there were no batteries inside of it.

A few weeks after the radio incident occurred, a ghost paid a visit to Steve's mom. Late one evening, she was sleeping in her bedroom and she was suddenly awakened by a cold breeze. When she opened her eyes, she observed a transparent head making its way around her bedroom. The head belonged to the ghost of an Indian. The ghost had long white hair and he was wearing a necklace. Steve's mom saw the stripes that were painted on the ghost of the Indian's face.

LEIGH AVENUE NEAR FOXWORTHY

Jan B. lived in a four-plex at 1222 Leigh Avenue. Jan was twenty years old and her friend's mother-in-law, Regina, passed away. Two days after Regina died, Jan was walking down the stairs and she was pushed on the chest by invisible hands.

Jan became frightened, but then she heard a voice inside of her head saying, "Stop and pay attention."

The ghost of Regina needed Jan's help retrieving the deed of trust for her house which she'd hidden under the carpet. Jan was told to go to the middle of the family room and find the deed of trust underneath the carpet. She did so, and one hour later, the family called on the phone asking Jan if she knew where the deed of trust was for Regina's property.

When Jan moved, the ghost of Regina followed her. And between 1974 and 1978, Regina visited Jan and helped take care of her daughter.

THE HAUNTED BURBANK NEIGHBORHOOD

Isabel Ramirez lives near Scott Street and I lived on Scott Street, back in 1987. Isabel and her family were watching television and they saw a shadow moving by the window. They assumed the shadow belonged to someone who was approaching the front door of the house. When Isabel looked out the window to see who was approaching the front door, she saw nobody.

Numerous times, they have seen the shadow, which belongs to a ghost. The door bell rang and Isabel quickly opened the front door. To her surprise, there was no one there and there was not enough time for a prankster to run away without being noticed.

Sometimes, Isabel's grand daughter stared out the back door as if she was looking at someone, but there never was anybody visible standing there.

Junior Ramirez lives in the same area, near San Jose City College. Junior's girlfriend was taking a shower and the bathroom door was locked. When she was out of the shower, she noticed a message written in the steam covering the bathroom mirror. The message said, "I am your mirror."

According to Junior, the hand writing on the mirror was nicer than any hand writing they were capable of creating. Junior's girlfriend lived in an apartment near the corner of Scott and Bascom Avenues. When Junior was sitting in the living room of her apartment, he heard the refrigerator door opening and closing when nobody was in the kitchen. Junior's girlfriend saw the ghost of a baby boy crying at the top of the stairs.

PETCO

Petco is a pet store that is located on Meridian Avenue near Branham Lane. An Alpha Beta grocery store used to occupy the building that Petco now occupies.

Gabriel was working at Petco when I was there shopping for cat food and he shared several ghost stories with me (including a story about a haunted house he used to live in). He informed me about some of the paranormal events that occurred inside store.

One day, there were three employees working. One of the employees walked back near the warehouse, while the other two employees were working towards the front of the store. Suddenly, every one heard a loud banging sound coming from the warehouse. The two employees near the front of the store assumed that their co-worker was in the warehouse and that she was responsible for noise they heard.

But she was not in the warehouse and she had nothing to do with the noise they heard. They never found out what caused the sound. Gabriel was in the pet washing section of the store which is on the left hand side of the building. The lights in that area were turning on and off by themselves. None of the pets appeared to be fazed by the haunting, including dogs that customers brought in to go shopping. (The store allows it's customers to bring their dogs inside the store to go shopping with them.)

During the month of November 2007, Jessica was working at Petco. It was night time, and Jessica saw a person standing in an isle of the store. She assumed that the person was one of her co-workers. But as she continued to approach the person, they suddenly vanished from her sight. Employees hear noises, and some employees are scared to go upstairs where a mostly vacant storeroom exists.

A HAUNTED APARTMENT
NEAR VALLEY MEDICAL CENTER

Denise Padia was born and raised in San Francisco, and that is where most of her hard core stories took place. But now she lives across the street from Valley Medical Center—and I have been there once.

Denise had a younger brother who passed away in 1991, and he is the reason for most of the paranormal experiences that she has had while living there. The curtains move around, the door shut twice by itself, and when she sat on her couch, she felt her hair being pulled.

Denise and her pet Chihuahua, Andrew Ray, were close. But unfortunately, Andrew Ray was hit and killed by a car that was driving down Moorpark Avenue. The next day, Denise heard the sound of Andrew Ray's bell and she felt him tugging on her pants. Denise used to spoil Andrew Ray and gave him small milk bones. When Andrew Ray was cremated, Denise included with the dog's body, a box of milk bones she had. Not long after the dog's funeral, Denise found a large sized milk bone on her carpet. The milk bone was bigger than the ones she used to give to Andrew Ray. Denise thinks the milk bone is a token of appreciation that was delivered by the ghost of her little dog.

THE ROSE GARDEN SECTION OF SAN JOSE

Susan Sablan lived in a haunted complex on Park and Hester Avenue, across the street from The Park & Hester Food and Liquor. Susan and other tenants heard the sounds of children running down the halls and playing. When people look in the hallways, there are no children present. The building still exists, but now serves as dental offices.

Dianne Cruz lives in the Rose Garden area and she was temporarily restrained by a ghost on one occasion. Dianne is under the impression that the ghost is a boy. Sometimes when she is in her bedroom with the door open, she sees a figure at the top of the stairs. Her house is old and she thinks the body of a child might be buried on the property, though she is not sure.

A friend of mine, named Ruben, recently moved into a house which is in the Rose Garden neighborhood. He heard the sound of disembodied breathing while he was walking in the hallway, early in the morning.

BERNIE'S HAUNTED HOUSE
NEAR THE VALLEY MEDICAL CENTER

Bernie is a co-worker of mine who lives near Valley Medical Center. He was at home changing light bulbs and went out the front door to put a brand new bulb inside of the socket. But when he turned on the light switch, the bulb blew out. Bernie went back inside to get another bulb and replaced another light bulb. The same thing happened again. The light bulb blew out when Bernie flipped the light switch on.

When the electricians arrived to his house, he said to them, "Check things out because weird things have been going on, including the door bell ringing on its own." After investigating the premises, the electricians did not detect any electrical problems.

Another time, Bernie was making some electrical repairs on his house and turned off the power to eliminate getting zapped. When he turned the power back on, various appliances were blinking off and on.

Bernie decided to set the clock on his microwave oven and he purposely set the clock four minutes fast for his son's sake. He was the only person inside the house. Later, still alone, he walked back into his bedroom and noticed the clock was blinking on and off, though it had previously been set. Bernie exited his room, but when he went back again a moment later, he noticed the clock was no longer blinking. The time on the clock was set *four minutes fast*.

PARANORMAL EXPERIENCES IN WILLOW GLEN

Sergio Perez and his family moved into a Willow Glen townhouse, back in 2004. Locked inside their storage area was a karaoke doll that sings along to music. The doll belongs to Sergio's wife and sometimes they heard the doll singing while it was being kept in their storage closet. Sergio was about to turn the button off, but before he could, the doll said, "See you later."

Sergio and his wife keep a collection of toy elephants on top of their refrigerator. While Sergio was using his computer to search for ghost stories in Mexico, an invisible force pushed every single one of the toy elephants off of the top of the appliance.

Sergio assumes there is the ghost of a girl hanging out inside of his place. The ghost likes to watch television and play with his daughter's toys. Sometimes, they find the toys moved from the place they were last set down.

Lots of things happened at the home. An orb appeared in a photograph taken of his daughter. At midnight, Sergio heard the sound of a door creaking, but when he checked around to see what was happening, he found all of the doors closed. The next thing he heard, on that same night, was the muffled sound of footsteps—he assumes the ghost was trying to walk quietly. On more than one occasion, the television was mysteriously turning on at 3 am and the volume was turned up loud. Sergio's wife thought the television noise was coming from their next door neighbor's place. Sergio also heard the sound of someone walking from the upstairs restroom to his son's room, where they tried opening the door (but the handle was locked).

Sergio's stepdaughter was friends with a guy by the name of Christian who attended Willow Glen High School. Unfortunately, he was murdered. The friendly ghost of Christian visited Sergio's stepdaughter, and she saw his face because he was peeking through a hole in the door that was missing a door knob. Sergio heard his stepdaughter crying and calling Christian's name. She moved out, but they still heard the sound of Christian lurking around the premises trying to find her.

On the kitchen table was a baby bottle in a cup holder. The cup holder slid across the kitchen table while Sergio stood there watching—he was shocked. Sergio moved the cup holder back to its original position and the cup started sliding by itself across the kitchen table. He moved the cup back again, and for the third time, the cup slid across the table.

He took a picture of the cup with his cell phone, and I haven't seen anything quite like this picture. The energy formed a pattern on the table top which resembled a ripple in water. Above the cup is a solid and thin white beam of energy in a vertical position.

AWAKENED BY A GHOST
NEAR MERIDIAN AND HILLSDALE AVENUES

Cassandra works at Andy's Pet Shop and she lives near Meridian and Hillsdale Avenue, which is next to the neighborhood I live in. She and some friends were sleeping in her room one night. On the following morning, the ghost of Cassandra's grandfather went around and slapped every single one of them on the side of the head. This was his effective, but ghostly method for waking them up.

An Angel at Jimmy's on Andalusia Drive

Jimmy Hunt's mom lives down the street from my family's house, on Andalusia Drive. Jimmy claims he was in his bed one evening when he saw an angel on the ceiling of his bedroom. The angel had a pleasant smile on her face and she soon disappeared.

Haunted Households of Willow Glen

Near Willow Glen High School

My sister had a friend by the name of Jennifer who lived near Willow Glen High School. Jennifer told my sister that a ghost followed her family from their old house to the one they were living in near the high school. The ghost was in her bedroom and sometimes in her closet.

Fairglen Drive

My parents are the original owners of their house on Fairglen Drive. I did not notice any paranormal activity occurring inside their house for many years. It seems as if strange things started happening there in the year of 2000.

I assume the minimal activity in my bedroom is attributed to a friend of mine who died. He appeared in a dream I had, and we spoke very briefly before my dream was over. Because of the dream and other factors, I have reason to believe his ghost has in fact visited my bedroom. I have two small brushes I use for my turntable needle. One day, I found both brushes underneath the two bases that support the right hand side of the turn table. My compact disc player also continued playing after I'd turned it off.

One year later, the same thing happened again. I pushed the stop button on the remote, but nothing happened. I pushed the power button on the player and I turned off the power. The song was still playing—and I stood up, ready to confront a ghost that might be present. I felt a weird vibe in the air for a moment. The compact disc player did not stop playing until I turned the receiver off. The disc player has been working fine ever since.

I was wearing my stereo headphones at night at one point. I went to the restroom and when I returned, I noticed my headphones had been unplugged. I found a bolt resting on one of my drum set's cymbals. The ghosts always do something noticeable, letting me know they were there.

My sister, Kathy, was working in the garage and the front door of the house was open. Kathy noticed someone running into the house and they closed the front door. She entered the house, went upstairs, and found her bedroom door closed. She heard a little bit of noise coming from inside of her bedroom and chose not go inside until later on that day.

Ashley is my oldest niece, and for two weeks, her bedroom window was being opened half way. Her bedroom is on the second level of the two-story house so we assume a ghost was responsible for opening her window.

During the month of October 2007, Ashley heard footsteps coming up the stairs at one a.m. She opened her door and looked to see who it was, but there was nobody standing there. Most likely a ghost was making its way up the stairs, and it may have been a relative watching over the family.

One evening, I found the downstairs bathroom door locked from the inside. And it can only be locked if someone goes inside the bathroom and closes the door all of the way.

Kiersten is my youngest niece and she was taking a picture of Ashley while they were in the family room. It was daytime and they were watching television when Kiersten took the photo with her cell phone camera. The dark and solid shadow of a boy ghost appeared in the picture. The ghost is in the back yard and he is looking in through the window of the sliding glass door. I have a brother that passed away before I was born. I wonder if it might be him in the picture?

Arroyo Seco Drive

Marcie M. is friends with my older sister and her mom's house was on Arroyo Seco Drive. Marcie mentioned the possibility of Indians being buried in that area of San Jose near Leigh Avenue. Her family lived in the house for twenty years and once in a while, furniture and other items went flying through the air of the room. Indian spirits could be the culprits for the paranormal activity they witnessed.

A Ghost in the Window

Teri V. told me a story about her friend's house having a ghost. Teri's friend lives in an apartment on top a garage which is located off Camden Avenue, near Highway 17. The ghost of a boy was seen looking out of an upstairs window. Unexplainable noises were heard, a watch disappeared, then came back, and a pair of socks that were on the couch twice moved onto the floor of the apartment.

Teri's friend was dropped off one evening and the people inside the car who dropped her off noticed someone was in the upstairs window. They waved, but the person in the window did not wave back. They thought Teri's friend had a rude roommate—but she did not have a roommate. The person they thought was a roommate was actually the ghost of a boy looking out the upstairs window. Perhaps the ghost is a boy who used to live on the property or nearby wishing he could ride along, too...

Oak Hill Cemetery

Oak Hill Cemetery is located on Monterey Road. I took quite a few pictures in the daytime, but there were no ghostly phenomena in any of the photos. An employee I met was going to share some ghost stories with me if I returned the following day. But when I returned, I was unable to find him. Still, because of the employee, I knew that there were stories to consider. I dug deeper.

Johnny Johnson is a co-worker of mine and he said, "Oak Hill Cemetery is a different place at night." Johnny's cousin is a security captain who patrols Oak Hill Cemetery. (I personally remember a security guard catching me and my friends inside the cemetery at night. He escorted us to the front gate and we were lucky he was a nice guy. Always beware the rules of a cemetery when you visit.) A lot of security guards quit because they hear voices or see a shadowy figure inside of the mausoleum at Oak Hill.

Dan was a security guard at Oak Hill Cemetery and David Derr knew him from the vitamin store at Valley Fair Shopping Mall. When Dan was patrolling the cemetery at night, he heard the sound of a baby crying while he was inside the mausoleum. He saw the ghosts of children playing in a circle.

Ray Castillo mentioned a ghost that haunts Oak Hill Cemetery as well. Ray said, "Almost every night, you can see the ghost of a man walking around the cemetery."

Brian Glenn worked at Oak Hill Cemetery but he was not scared of working among all of the dead bodies being prepared for burial. There was one occasion, however, when Brian felt as if an ice-cold finger was poking into his back and touching his spine. He never felt anything like it before, and for the first time, Brian was scared while he was on duty at Oak Hill.

Another story I heard goes like this: A guy was driving by Oak Hill Cemetery at night and he picked up a lady who was hitchhiking. They went dancing and he let her wear his jacket. Afterwards, she wanted to be dropped back off at the cemetery. She ran into the cemetery and he went looking for her. He found his jacket. It was sitting on top of her tombstone.

Do ghosts in fact return to their graves? The word is, Marilyn Monroe has appeared hovering near her grave in Westwood... So maybe the same thing happens here at Oak Hill.

A HAUNTED COFFEE SHOP

Down the street from Oak Hill Cemetery is Starbucks on Monterey Road. An employee by the name of Devora informed me of some paranormal activity which took place inside the coffee shop. A couple of day-shift employees were on duty at 5 am and they noticed the drive-through window opening by itself. Also, bags of coffee grinds fall down from a shelf and have to be picked up off the floor and put back. An employee at the shop came up with an extravagant name for the ghost—something like Mary Antoinette.

If the ghost is not of a person who lived on the site that Starbucks occupies, the ghost might be someone who lived where other buildings are standing in the same shopping center. There are houses and a mobile home park in the area. Also in that area is a house behind the fairgrounds that is notorious for being haunted. Could this be the source of the Starbucks ghostly visitors?

A co-worker of mine told me about the house, but I was unable to locate the property when I went looking for it. There is a small two-story house behind the fairgrounds that has a fence around it, and the place appears to be abandoned. Perhaps this is the haunted house I heard about and nobody lives inside it any more—it's the scariest looking house on the street. And maybe the ghost there is thirsty for a really good latté from time to time.

Chapter Eight:
UNFRIENDLY GHOSTS
OF SAN JOSE

REXFORD WAY

I sincerely believe that most of the ghosts in San Jose are friendly, but there are some unfriendly ones that I hear about from time to time. Emma Davis lived in an apartment complex on Rexford Avenue, near Valley Medical Center. She picked up some food from Jack in the Box and drove back to the development. It was night time when Emma parked her car; then she walked up the driveway which was dark because the light bulb was out.

Standing there, with his back facing Emma, was a creepy-looking man with long hair, long fingernails, and wearing a black trench coat. Emma said, "Excuse me; can I help you."

He did not respond and Emma felt she had better keep on moving. She ran upstairs, locked the door, then she called a friend who arrived in ten minutes. There was no trace of the man Emma saw in front of the complex. He was gone.

But this was not the only strange thing occurring for Emma.

She and her friend witnessed plenty of ghost activity in her apartment and they were both screaming at times when the situation was frightening. Emma had beads hanging from a doorway and the beads began swinging without being touched. They heard the ghost running across the room and into the bathroom. They even heard the sound of it breathing.

One time, Emma dozed off with her arms stretched out. She was awakened by her hand being squeezed. She noticed her bed move down from the weight of the ghost upon it and she felt the ghost climb into bed with her, then put its arm around her. She was unable to move or scream for a little while. As soon as she was able to scream again, she yelled at the ghost and called it terrible names. Emma's raging fit was effective and the ghost did not mess with her again.

BUCKESTO PARK

Henry Jacobo lived on Tenth Street near Empire Street. Henry, along with eleven friends, were drinking warm beer as they made their way to Buckesto Park on Thirteenth Street. Eventually, some of the guys passed out or took off and there were only three guys remaining in the park. Henry, Bill, and Louie were still sipping beer and hanging out.

They noticed a woman in a dress on one of the swings. She was crying, and Bill wanted to see if he could cheer her up—and possibly get lucky with her. Bill approached the swings as Henry and Louie watched. Bill walked up to the lady and he put his hand on her shoulder. She turned her head towards him and he immediately turned pale. He instantly knew something was wrong and it was time to start running.

Henry never ran four blocks so fast in his life. Bill and Louie were following him and the ghost was following the three of them. Henry ran home and hid under his bed. His mom had to bring home a catholic priest in order to persuade him to come out from under the bed. He missed school for three days and so did Bill and Louie.

Bill was not quite sure what he saw when he looked at the ghost's face. "The three of us had the same dream, but it was not a dream," Henry said.

A MALEVOLENT GHOST NEAR V.M.C.

Tu Tran and his family live off Fruitdale Avenue, not far from Emma's old place on Rexford Avenue. Tu had an unfriendly ghost lingering inside his apartment and the ghost may have followed his family from their residence in Milpitas. We originally assumed the ghost might have been emotionally attached to the bedroom set in their home, possibly because she used to own the set. But the Trans still had some trouble after they sold it.

Tu's wife was on the right-hand side of their bed sleeping and she woke up yelling. Tu was afraid of the neighbors hearing her voice, so he told her to be quiet. The problem was, a ghost was restraining her and she felt as if she was being strangled.

Tu felt helpless during the ordeal which lasted one minute. After having this happen three nights in a row, Tu and his wife changed their sleeping positions. Tu was now sleeping on the right-hand side of the bed and he became a victim of what ghost hunters call old hag syndrome. A malevolent ghost sits on top of someone, or they hold the person down. They also temporarily paralyze their victim's vocal chords, preventing them from yelling or screaming for help.

Another day, Tu was resting and he heard a noise; then he was unable to move or scream for a matter of seconds. Tu and his wife did not affiliate the bad nightmares with the bedroom set until Tu took a picture of the furniture in an attempt to sell it. The ghost of a lady wearing a veil appeared in the picture. While remaining invisible in front of the bedroom set mirror, her solid reflection was cast against the mirror.

Mike K. practices Feng Shui and he was a janitor at a local electronics company. Ghostly activity was not new to him. He brought his boom box to work with him to listen to music while he worked. When Mike went into another room, he no longer heard the music because a ghost turned his radio off. He turned the radio back on, and when he exited the room, the volume went up. And sometimes the volume was turned down when Mike was cleaning in the next room.

Mike visited Tu's apartment and gave Tu advice about how to deal with the situation. Mike insisted that Tu get rid of the bedroom set and that Tu burn the picture of the ghost. Tu also rearranged the furniture in his house per Mike's suggestion. People rearrange their furniture hoping ghosts will not recognize where they are and will leave because the place does not look familiar to them. Mike did what he could, but the ghost was still hanging around.

Tu came to work and said to me, "Hey David. I had a picture of a ghost, but I already burned it."

I replied, "You destroyed a picture of a ghost without letting me check it out first? You know that is my line of work!" Thankfully, Tu still had the negatives in his possession and he gave them to me.

As activity continued, it was decided that further measures were necessary. The first priest who came over to cleanse Tu's place was from Milpitas and Tu paid him $300 to clear the home. Tu had an altar in his apartment for religious purposes. The priest mostly focused on that area and the problems stopped for approximately three months. But it didn't end there.

A second priest was paid $300 and he acknowledged the presence of three spirits that were near Tu's altar—two adults and one child. It was time to move! So, Tu's family moved into the apartment next door. Unfortunately, the ghost was able to find them there.

One evening, Tu was about to leave the home and his family was waiting for him in the car. He turned around to shut the door, but the door had already been closed (by the ghost). It was then that Tu heard the sound of someone inside the apartment knocking on the other side of his front door. Tu decided to get into his car and drive away.

Tu was working in the diet office at Valley Medical Center on a Thursday afternoon. He decided to call home because he wanted to know how his son (Darryl) was doing. Daryl had a doctor's appointment at 2 pm that day. Tu figured that his wife, his son, and his daughter (Sabrina) should have been home by three-thirty p.m. When he called home, he heard the voice of Sabrina answer the phone. In the background it sounded as if Daryl was crying and Tu's wife was trying to comfort him.

Tu asked Sabrina, "May I speak to Mom?" Sabrina is kind of shy and normally it would be like her to hand the phone to her mother, right away. But this time, Tu was surprised when Sabrina said, "Mom is busy giving Daryl a bath. Why don't you call back, Dad?" Tu was shocked at

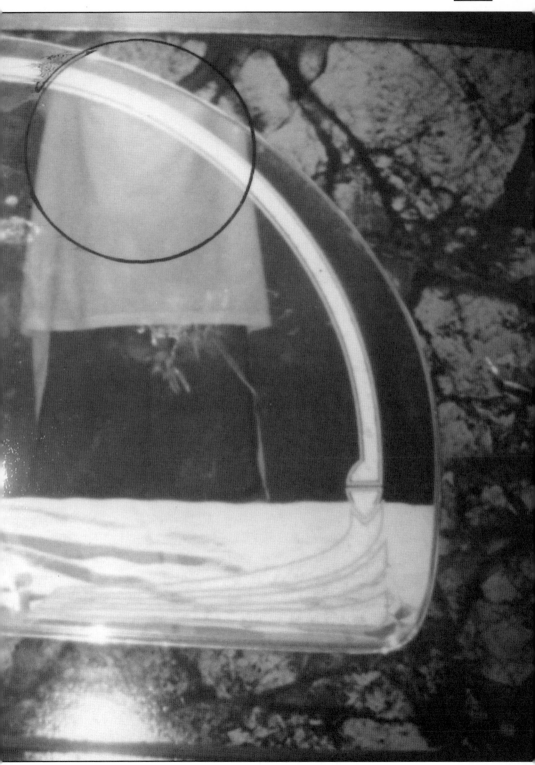

A malevolent ghost in the mirror of Tu Tran's apartment. *Courtesy of Tu Tran.*

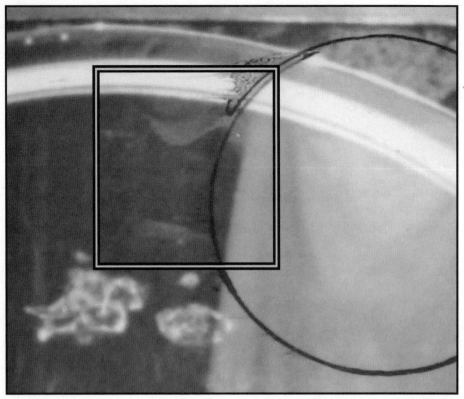

Detail of previous photo.

his daughter's tone and response. But he figured, she was just a child and he said, "All right Sabrina. I'll call her back later." Sabrina replied, "Okay Dad," in a tone that was almost a giggle.

Tu thought it was strange. His daughter usually did not giggle like that. But then again, Tu thought to himself, "It is not a big deal. Sabrina is only a kid." He called back at 4 pm and the telephone rang for a while; then his wife answered and she was out of breath. Tu's wife explained to him that she and the kids had just walked through the door of their apartment. They'd finally arrived home from the doctor's office.

Tu said, "What are you talking about? When I called at three-thirty, Sabrina told me that you were busy with Daryl and she asked me to call back later."

Tu's wife replied, "Well you know how long of a wait it is to see a doctor. We just arrived home a minute ago."

He asked if she was sure and she said, "I would know if we arrived home at three-thirty. And I know a half hour is not enough time for me to complete the errands I had to run." So, who had he spoken to on the phone?

Three days later, Tu came home from work at seven-ten p.m. His wife told him that her mom claimed she'd called two times long distance from Japan. But someone not of the family had been answering the phone. Her mom said she called at 5 pm and spoke with Sabrina. The child was rude to her and said, "You call too much. Why don't you hang up the phone and shut up?" The ghost that haunts Tu's apartment was imitating Sabrina's voice on the telephone.

And so it was that a third priest from San Francisco was paid $500 to get rid of the ghost at Tu's place. He burned incense, had beads on his wrist, and blessed the entire apartment. When the priest was through, three black marks appeared on the palm of his hand. The three black stripes, which could not be rubbed off, represented each of the three spirits. The marks went away after the priest prayed for a while.

Tu and his family have not had any problems since.

A Ghost in a Tree Berryessa

Tu's brother lived in Berryessa, back in '97. His brother had a roommate who saw a light shining through his window on some nights. He used to get up, look out the window, and see a ghost sitting on a tree branch. He was alarmed and, at one point, covered his window with tin foil. Every time Tu spent the night at the house, he experienced old hag syndrome. He hardly ever spent the night at the house anymore.

Perhaps the property was haunted by former tenants who felt as if their privacy was being invaded—or maybe there's more to this family tree than anyone suspected…

The Haunted House Nobody Lives In
Senter and Hellyer Avenues

Tu was the first person to tell me about the house on the corner of Senter and Hellyer Avenues. He said the house was haunted and was popular among members of the Vietnamese community.

Betty Z. was the next person to tell me about the house. I heard stories about the place being haunted by a mean ghost and that people who move into the house end up dying.

Emma Davis had a friend who hunted ghosts. He talked about a haunted house in the Evergreen area and I'm not sure if it was this particular house, but it was close enough to consider. Supposedly, even a cop died inside the house. It is said that people either die or disappear if they go inside it.

Teri V. told me how to find the house, and I could tell when I found it that there was nobody staying there. Teri does not know for sure if it is true, but she heard a story about a man who was dared to spend the night inside the house on Hellyer Avenue. He accepted the challenge

A haunted house on Hellyer Avenue. The ghost has control of the place.

and it backfired. The guy was found naked on the front lawn, the following morning.

I placed a letter in the mailbox of the house, but I was never contacted by the owner to hear further information. The ghost holding down the fort is most likely a former owner who paid for the house, and, as far as the ghost is concerned, the house still belongs to it—and it has no intention of sharing the residence with living tenants.

OUIJA BOARD SESSION GONE BAD IN EAST SAN JOSE

Adriana is a county employee and she lived in East San Jose. She purchased a Ouija board as a birthday gift for a friend. Her sister and her friends begged her to open the package so they could play with the board. At first, Adriana refused because it was a birthday present. But she finally gave in, opened up the box, and took the board out.

Adriana and her sister's friend had their hands on the planchette and it started moving around, but not spelling words. It began moving out of control so they took their hands off, but the planchette continued to move around on its own. They put their hands back on top of the planchette, to try to stop it from moving.

It was then that Adriana's spirit was pushed out of her body and up into a corner near the ceiling of the room. She was above and looking down at herself and the other two girls. The voice of her body below changed and it was deeper. The voice began to swear horribly at her sister and her sister's friend. The ghost had taken control of Adriana's body.

She saw and heard everything that was happening, but there was nothing she could do to stop the situation as she lingered in the corner of the room as an invisible presence. Adriana said horrible words that she normally would not have said, including the questions, "Why are you doing this to me? What do you want?"

All of the commotion had caused Adriana's parents to get out of bed to see what in the world was going on. Her parents entered the bedroom and her father tried to calm who they thought was their daughter. She lunged towards her father and the others tried to restrain her. Adriana's mom exited the room to go to get her rosary beads and holy water. When she returned to Adriana's bedroom, she threw water onto Adriana and the activity suddenly ceased.

The predicament finally ended and Adriana's soul went back inside her body. She sat there and cried. The rosary beads and the holy water seemed to make a difference.

One problem with using a Ouija board is the fact that you don't know who the ghost is that's communicating with you.

PLEASANT ECHO DRIVE

When John Viray lived on Pleasant Echo Drive, he was subdued by a ghost on two different occasions. The first time John had experienced old hag syndrome, he was sleeping in his bedroom with the curtains closed. John's room was dark and that never helps in a frightening situation. When he woke up, it felt as if his blanket was being held down and he could hardly move. The temporary restraining ended a minute later. One year later, the same thing happened. Except this time, John was more alert and focused on trying to move his hands and his feet. He was unable to move or scream for one minute before turning the light on inside his room. Fortunately, this frightening experience never happened to John again. Though there is indeed a sleep disorder that can cause paralysis, John is convinced that this was something much more malevolent. Old Hag Syndrome is nothing to sneeze at.

VICTIM OF A CURSE LONGMEADOW DRIVE

When Connie O. lived on Longmeadow Drive, she was the victim of a hex placed on her. Connie does not talk about the turmoil she went through very often. It's not a good idea to bring the matter up for discussion. The curse included the evil spirit of a child who had more or less attached himself to Connie's back. She actually felt the extra weight on her back and felt fatigued, all of the time.

Connie needed help, and two ladies who are specialists, arrived from Mexico to take care of the problem she was having. The ladies performed an exorcism, which included prayer. They saw the spirit of a bad child and the spirit of a good child who was trying to deter the bad spirit that was pestering Connie. They were able to get rid of the unwanted spirit that was helping to fulfill a curse. The ladies concluded that, most likely, Connie's wicked stepmother was the one who placed the curse on her. She was born in El Salvador, and she lived in Los Angeles where she passed away. Connie's stepmother did not like Connie.

A THREATENING GHOST
IN EAST SAN JOSE

Maria was an employee who used to work at Valley Medical Center. She was taking care of her dying mother at home.

Maria's sister-in-law was a negative person when she was alive and now she exists as a miserable ghost. Her ghost told Maria, "I'll kill you and your mother."

The ghost did not attack either of them, but she made threats which served to keep everyone's nerves on end.

Maria's mom did eventually die, but peacefully. A lady I work with saw a picture of her ghost because it appeared in a mirror while the photo was being taken.

A GHOST HOLDING A KNIFE
NEAR CAPITOL EXPRESSWAY AND MCKEE ROAD

Manuel Barragan and his family, for sixteen years, lived in a haunted house near Capitol Expressway and Mckee Road. A man died in the living room of the house and he might be the ghost involved. Although nobody was ever harmed, Manuel considered the ghost to be unfriendly. Sometimes, Manuel found himself fighting with a family member while driving in his car and approaching the house. He was under the impression that living in that house caused him and his family to be in bad moods.

And there were other signs. Manuel's family heard noises in the attic, resembling the sounds of someone walking on the wooden beams. One night, his father-in-law observed the ghost of a man in the house. It was holding a knife in its hand. The ghost walked from the living room to the kitchen, to the back door, and then disappeared in the back yard.

Manuel removed a heater from the wall between the kitchen and a bedroom. Inside the wall, he found an old newspaper from the late 1800s. The old newspaper contained information pertaining to the man who used to own the house. According to the paper, the man died in the living room.

Manuel's wife had an old-fashioned sewing machine in one of the rooms. Late one evening, Manuel and his family heard a loud crashing sound and they assumed the sewing machine fell and hit the floor. To their surprise, nothing was disturbed when they checked out the sewing machine and the room where it sat.

Manuel and his family would probably still own that house if there wasn't a ghost there!

GHOSTS ON LUPTON AVENUE

I met Ryan M. at Martini Brothers Bar, in downtown San Jose. Ryan's family lived in a house on Lupton Avenue near Minnesota Avenue. Ten people were murdered on his family's block. Barbara Green was the name of the lady who used to live in the house that Ryan's family occupied for one hundred years. Barbara shot her husband dead, then shot and killed herself.

Ryan considered her to be an unfriendly ghost. His great grandmother was dying and she told Ryan's family that there was a lady trying to kill her. Objects flew across rooms, lights turned on and off on their own, and a rocking chair moved by itself, blocking the doorway entrance to part of the house that was added on. At least six people saw the ghost of Barbara Green, including Ryan's mom, his sister, and his brother.

Ryan also saw the ghost of Mr. Green countless times. The ghost of Mr. Green appeared in the backyard and Ryan used to see him waving, though he did not know who the ghost was waving to.

When Ryan's family was moving out of the house on Lupton Avenue, there was a dumpster sitting in front. On the ground near the dumpster was a photograph that appeared untouched. The picture was of the house before Ryan's family moved there some one hundred years ago. It was blurry and there were people shown. It gave them the creeps and they immediately discarded it. Ryan was under the impression that it was impossible for the picture to exist. He could not believe the picture found did not even have a speck of dust on it, although it was next to a dumpster and the place was a mess. The picture seemed to appear from nowhere. Did a ghost produce the photo?

The next family that moved into the house on Lupton Avenue moved out only six months later. The house was finally demolished and a new house was built on the site.

SCRATCHED BY A GHOST

Priscilla Fuentes used to work for the County of Santa Clara. At her uncle's house, a group of people were using a Ouija board. Even though Priscilla's uncle was not one of the people using the board, he is the one who was attacked by a demonic spirit because of it. There were scratches resembling claw marks that appeared on his arm.

The Ouija board session probably provoked an unfriendly spirit who took its aggression out on Priscilla's uncle.

On a lighter note, after her uncle's dog died, the dog's ghost appeared in a photo someone took on the property.

HIT & RUN BY A GHOST
NEAR STOKES AVENUE

Isabel Ramirez has been a co-worker of mine for a long time and thanks to her, I met her son and interviewed him. If Junior's story is not my favorite, it is definitely one of my favorites. He and his friend were driving in Junior's car near Stokes Avenue when a lady's car hit his car. Attempting a hit and run, the lady stepped on the gas and was fleeing from the scene of the accident.

Junior followed after the lady yelling, "You are going to pay for this!" He caught up with the lady's car, and as Junior was driving on the side of her vehicle, he looked over and was surprised to see that the lady now appeared to look like a bear.

It sounds to me like Junior was the hit-and-run victim of a demonic shape shifter. Junior's friend saw the same thing—it looked like a bear was driving the other car! They followed the car to a shopping center on the corner of Leigh Avenue and Southwest Expressway. The bear lady's car ran into a dead end and Junior parked his car so that hers was boxed in.

She stepped on the accelerator and her car headed straight for Junior's car. He thought the lady was going to smash her car into his, causing a head on collision. Junior turned to his friend and said, "Get out of the car! She's going to ram us!" They both hurried out of his vehicle as the lady was speeding towards them.

But before the car smashed into Junior's, she and her car disappeared into thin air.

Junior's friend was convinced that someone put a hex on Junior. And he was no longer willing to hang out with him. And maybe I agree…

Chapter Nine:
SPECTERS
OF SOUTH SAN JOSE

GHOST ENCOUNTERS IN BLOSSOM HILL

When Cathy Zitzer was twelve years old, she lived near Oak Grove High School in South San Jose. Cathy felt scared while her family lived in that house. Late at night, when she was trying to go to sleep, she saw two ghosts standing in her dark bedroom. The ghosts used to stand near the end of her bed, draped in black. Cathy was unable to see their faces and she did not know if they were males or females. She was fully awake during these experiences and these ghosts scared her to death.

Cathy not only saw the ghosts, she felt their presences—a negative vibe coming from these two uninvited night-time visitors. But, as far as I know, they did not harm her—at least she did not mention it.

Cathy lived in another South San Jose house which was haunted by the ghost of a girl who was raped and murdered in the early seventies. Her body was found under a tree across the street from the house Cathy lived in. Cathy is unsure if the girl lived in the house her family occupied, or if she lived in the house across the street where her lifeless body was found.

Doors inside her house used to close by themselves. Out of the corner of her eye, she saw the shadowy figure of a ghost. One day, she found the toilet paper was pulled all the way out of the bathroom and down the hallway of their house.

GHOSTS IN THE MIRROR
NEAR BLOSSOM HILL ROAD AND SNELL AVENUE

A county employee by the name of Anna has a sister who lives in a condominium near Blossom Hill Road and Snell Avenue. Anna gave her sister a large-sized mirror because she did not have enough room in her house to keep it. The sister placed the mirror on the floor of her condominium, near the fireplace and took a photograph of her daughter while she was standing in front of it. When she developed the film, she was shocked to see the ghosts of seven people appear in the mirror. One of the specters was a man holding the ghost of a baby. Maybe these spirits were former tenants who resided on the property where condos now exist, or maybe they are just phantom visitors passing through the household.

The Ghost of a Pilot
Felder Drive

Norman Canady lived in a house on Felder Drive in South San Jose haunted by the ghost of a black man who was a helicopter pilot. The pilot had died in a helicopter crash. Norman's wife saw the ghost of the pilot moving down the hall of their house. His legs were crossed which meant that he was not walking—he was floating down the hallway. He noticed that Norman's wife was watching him and he tried to hide from her.

The ghost of the pilot was coming by at night to have a little bit of fun, scaring Norman's daughter, though there was no real harm being done. Norman's nephew had burned a hole in his daughter's blanket with a cigarette lighter. At night time when the ghost of the pilot was in her bedroom, Norman's daughter would peak through the hole in her blanket to see if the ghost was coming to get her. It would come right up to her. And, as she looked through the hole in her blanket, his hand would be right there—it was truly evident that he was having fun scaring her.

Norman eventually saw the ghost and he tried to have the house blessed, but the cleansing did not work. They ended up having to move out. When they were moving their belongings out, the ghost slammed the door behind them. Norman thinks the ghost was glad they were moving.

Rocket Fuel and Ghosts
Off Metcalf Road

Michael H. was a security guard who was assigned to guard a corporation called Pratt Whitney, located off Metcalf Road in South San Jose. Rocket fuel was made at Pratt Whitney and they'd had an accidental fire or two. Before the place was eventually shut down, some of the security guards who used to guard Pratt Whiney saw ghosts. Michael H. never stumbled upon a ghost, but other security guards who patrolled the surrounding fields of the property encountered the spirit of an Indian riding a horse. The ghost of the Indian waved hello to the guards who saw him and his horse. Indians inhabited that area of San Jose, years ago.

Visited by a Deceased Friend
Saratoga

Jim Sullivan owns a bar in Saratoga called The Bank. Hanging on the back wall of the bar next to the restrooms is a picture of a man bartending. The bartender is wearing a wrist watch and a white shirt. But his head did not appear in the photo. The bartender may even be Jim or his father, who is still alive. Is the bartender Jim or his father (who is still alive) or does this photo represent something more ghostly? I don't know. A guy in the bar said it was a ghost, but it looks like the bartender is Jim's size...

Around forty years ago, Jim had a best friend who died. The next day after his friend's funeral, Jim was driving his car down Blossom Hill Road in South San Jose. Jim thinks he may have seen the ghost of his best friend appear in the passenger seat of his car for a split second. Jim is very skeptical and he struggles to believe that the ghost of his best friend was actually riding in the car with him as he was driving. Countless people have been visited by the ghosts of close friends.

GHOSTS WATCH OVER THEIR LOVED ONES NEAR ALMADEN EXPRESSWAY

Chrissie Smith, C.N.A., works at the same hospital I do. Chrissie's grandmother passed away on March 26, 2004. Evidently, the ghost of Chrissie's beloved followed her to a bridal shop near Almaden Expressway in South San Jose, six months later.

Chrissie does not like the color gold, but her Grandmother did, and her grandmother owned a lot of gold jewelry. When Chrissie was choosing a wedding dress, she never dreamed she would end up buying a gold dress. But there was just such a dress in the shop that stood out among the rest. She tried it on and her mom was there taking pictures of the event.

Chrissie was standing in front of some mirrors when she noticed one of her mom's pictures was different from the rest. This particular photograph showed a white cloud above Chrissie and the ghost of Chrissie's grandmother standing in front of one of the mirrors.

They showed the picture to Chrissie's fourteen-year-old daughter and she started to cry at the treasured image. If you study the picture, you will notice the ghost of Chrissie's grandmother is facing towards Chrissie's mom.

Before she passed away, Chrissie's grandmother was concerned about Chrissie having a husband and being taken care of. Her grandmother no longer has to worry about that. Maybe Chrissie chose a gold-colored dress that day because her grandmother's ghost was there to share the day with her.

THE GHOST OF TOMMY BLOSSOM HILL ROAD

Aloha Roller Rink was located on Blossom Hill Road in South San Jose. It opened for business in the late seventies, and in the early eighties, it was the place to be. I remember some of the good times my friends and I had at the roller rink.

The roller rink is now called San Jose Skate. Sam J. at The Improv is the one who provided a story for me about the roller rink having a ghost. A boy by the name of Tommy was inside San Jose Skate playing a game

San Jose Skate is haunted by the ghost of a boy.

of hide and go seek. Tommy was trying to find a good place to hide near the skate rental section but, unfortunately, he accidentally fell into a trash can that was full of water. Tommy drowned and they did not know where he was until they found his lifeless body, two days later.

Late at night, employees have seen shadows of the ghost, and lights were switching on and off by themselves. Sam is more skeptical than I am and I can't say that I have tougher standards than he does when it comes to authenticating a reported ghost sighting.

Sam's friend was working on the floor inside the rink at two in the morning in 2006, watching for the ghost of Tommy. His friend was busy working on the floor. Sam looked around for a while, but he did not see the ghost, so he turned to his friend and said, "I don't see the ghost." Sam's friend said, "Keep watching." Sam continued to look for the ghost and finally he saw the dark shadow of the ghost moving around.

According to Sam, there are three types of ghosts: Human, inhuman, and elemental—human ghosts which are people, inhuman which are animals and objects, and elemental which include sounds of the past being replayed by the atmosphere. Sam is one of the most hard-core guys I interviewed.

So, I wonder if there are ghosts roller skating at the rink?

FRIGHTENED IN THE OUTHOUSE
COYOTE CREEK

Petra Wright's mom lives in South San Jose near IBM. The house she lives in is old and there is an outhouse located at the back of the house. Coyote Creek is next to the property and the outhouse in the backyard is not far away from the creek.

As Petra's mom was using the outhouse, she heard the voice of a woman crying. She thought her sister was playing a joke on her, but her sister was not around. The crying she heard came from the creek. She wondered if it was the ghost of La Llorona, because her ghost is rumored to be traveling creeks, searching for the souls of her three children whom she drowned. According to Richard Senate's book, some people believe that La Llorona has killed people, including some children (Senate, 1986, 45).

A GHOST THREW A SHOE
SOUTH SAN JOSE

Santos is an employee I met at Andy's Pet Shop and he lives in South San Jose. Santos has a sister, and when he was seven years old, she asked him to go into her room to get her red sweater. Santos went into the room and picked up the sweater. No sooner than he'd picked it up, his nephew's shoe was thrown at him, hitting him on his back. Santos thought his dad was having fun with him. But when he turned around to see who had thrown the shoe, there was nobody else in his sister's bedroom. Santos dropped the sweater, ran out of the room, and told his sister to get the sweater herself.

His mom's father passed away and his ghost still follows them around the house. They see the silhouette of his grandfather's ghost on the anniversary of his death wearing a trench coat—and the whole family has seen him. His ghost is watching over the family.

A GHOST ATTENDS A FAMILY REUNION
HELLYER PARK

Nina Gaeta was at Hellyer Park attending a family reunion. Her deceased husband had a cousin by the name of Billy, and as Nina was walking around at the reunion, she saw Billy sitting at one of the picnic tables. Billy stood up from the table and walked over to Nina, gave her a hug, and said hello. After Billy walked away, Nina said to a relative, "I just saw Billy." They asked, "Billy who?" Nina said, "Cousin Billy." They said, "No you didn't. Billy has been dead for ten years."

Nina looked over to the spot where Billy was sitting at the picnic table. He was no longer there.

OBJECTS FLEW OUT OF THE CLOSET
NEAR ALMADEN EXPRESSWAY

Manuel Barragan moved to South San Jose and lives in a house near Almaden Expressway. When Manuel began telling me stories about his new house being haunted, I wondered if the ghost of his father-in-law was at his home, conducting pranks as usual.

Manuel was working on his car stereo and the roll of electrical tape he was using disappeared. He looked all over for it, but did not find it until the next day—sitting on the back seat of his car.

Manuel was resting one day. When he awakened, he noticed a piece of paper sitting next to him. Somehow, the ghost had taken the paper out of his wallet without him noticing. Another time, he was inside his house watching television. The ghost decided to throw some objects out of the closet. Out came a can of hairspray and a can of shoe polish. Manuel picked up the cans and placed them back inside the closet. Forty seconds later, a shoe box sitting behind the cans lifted up over the cans and flew out of the closet.

The prank-playing ghost is most likely a former resident who lived in the house or the ghost of a relative.

A HAUNTED DRUG STORE
NEAR ALMADEN EXPRESSWAY

Patty is a lady who told me about a drug store near Almaden Expressway having a ghost. Her friend's son was delivering Coca-Cola to the drugstore and he told an employee about a weird vibe he was sensing. The employee revealed to him that the store had a ghost.

Jan has worked at the drug store for twenty years, and she requested that I not mention the name of the drug store. It's a corporation I once worked for. The ghost has been haunting the store since 1997. They have no idea who the ghost is or where it came from.

I told Jan, "The ghost might have died in the house across the street and he comes by to visit."

A girl who works at the store decided to name the ghost Sebastian Walker. In general, the employees do not fear the ghost because he is playful. The ghost appears to be five feet tall, in his late twenties, and has blond hair. There is no specific time as far as when employees see or hear the ghost of Sebastian. Jan and one other employee have seen him, but they have not seen his face because, usually, his back is turned and they see him from a distance.

Jan has seen the ghost four times, and he moves chairs around in the upstairs part of the store's warehouse. Sebastian has been known to hang out in the receiving department of the drug store.

A grocery store used to be located on the property, years ago. Perhaps there was a farm house before the grocery store existed and that's where Sebastian originated from. One night, he helped Jan because the lights weren't properly set for daylight savings time. A timer went off, the lights went out, and Jan was all the way in the back of the pitch-black store's warehouse—she could not see a thing. Certainly, she would have not been able to make her way to the front of the store without walking into a pole or some other object. The ghost of Sebastian guided Jan to the store front by pushing her forward. Jan felt peace upon her as Sebastian was assisting her.

THE BERNAL GULNAC JOICE RANCH
SANTA CLARA COUNTY PARK

Terri Sanisio told me about Bernal-Gulnac-Joice Ranch having ghosts. John Dorrance is in charge of the historic Santa Clara County Park which includes: the Bernal ranch house, an open barn display, an Ohlone Indian burial ground, and Santa Theresa Spring (also known as Dottie's Pond). In 1834, the Mexican government granted nearly 10,000 acres of land to Jose Joaquin Bernal. Today, the ranch consists of twenty remaining acres on Manila Drive, near Santa Theresa Hospital. In 1860, the four-room ranch house was built, and ninety years later, the house increased in size. The Bernal family lived in the ranch house and operated the cattle ranch for more than one hundred years.

The Bernal House was certified as haunted.

Mary Bernal was a nurse at Valley Medical Center. John D. has worked at the park for a number of years and has not noticed any ghost activity inside of the ranch house, where his office is located. Gloria, who heads an organization called Ghost Trackers, conducted an investigation inside of the Bernal Ranch house. She and another lady stayed until two a.m. They investigated the house, using a micro cassette recorder, infra-red cameras, etc. Evidently, a ghost was detected because they either caught one on film, or captured an EVP, as they recorded a ghost's voice on tape.

I have never seen a certified haunted location before stepping into John's office. The Ghost Trackers organization presented John with a certificate stating that the Bernal ranch house was haunted. The lady who was filling in for John showed me the certificate hanging in his office. I thought, though, that the ranch house looked and felt as if a ghost was present. If in fact the ranch house is haunted, the ghost or ghosts are probably members of the Bernal family. The ranch house is ideal for ghosts because no one resides there and John D. is only there for eight hours during the week.

DOTTIE'S POND
SANTA CLARA COUNTY PARK

There is an interesting story about how the Santa Theresa Spring originated. The local Ohlone Indians were sick and needed help. So, they gathered around a spot where the pond is now located and they looked to the skies for help. Chief Umunhum, making one last attempt to summon for help, shot into the sky an arrow with a feather tied to it. Supposedly, the spirit of a lady wearing a black gown descended from the sky to help the Indians. In her hand was a crucifix that she struck against a rock and the spring came to exist. Every year, masses were held at the spring on October 15th.

The spring is also known as Dottie's Pond because Dottie is the name of a girl who allegedly committed suicide by drowning herself in the pond. Her ghost now haunts the pond. According to John D., the dead body of a girl was never found in the water. John says he is more likely to believe the story about the Ohlones being visited and saved by a lady from the sky. John has patrolled the area for years. He went swimming in Dottie's Pond and he's pulled items out of the pond, including a wheelchair. (I would not go swimming in Dottie's Pond unless you paid me greatly to do so.)

On Friday night November 16, 2007, David Derr and I investigated Dottie's Pond to decide for ourselves if the pond was haunted by a ghost. Kids who live in the neighborhood next to the pond have told John's substitute ranger about the pond having one. David and I arrived at the pond around eleven p.m., and during the first forty minutes of our stay, nothing happened. We began hearing noises during the last twenty minutes of our investigation, though. An acorn fell from a tree and hit the wooden walkway hard, as if someone had thrown it down from the tree. We saw the bushes moving in front of us, as if someone was walking by. I became alarmed. I took a step back and nearly ran out of the area.

David and I rarely run out of a place due to the presence of a ghost. We heard noises in back of us and did not notice any animals walking around. David heard the sound of footsteps on the other side of a fence he was standing next to. David almost took off running, and I'm under the impression that both of us were convinced there was a ghost haunting the pond.

If you decide to explore Dottie's Pond, don't worry about being harmed by the ghost of Dottie—be concerned about being harmed by rattlesnakes and mountain lions that live in the area.

THE HAYES MANSION
200 EDENVALE ROAD

The Hayes Mansion has a reputation for being haunted. In the 1970s, a co-worker of mine used to sneak into the mansion because it was abandoned at the time. His son used to sneak into the mansion in the 80s. The mansion is located at 200 Edenvale Avenue, near Monterey Road. Frontier Village amusement park operated next to the mansion and I remember enjoying Frontier Village when I was a kid, back in the '70s.

Norman Canady heard stories about people seeing the ghosts of gunfighters inside Frontier Village, which, unfortunately, was torn down. The Hayes Mansion was built by Mary Chynoweth Hayes, in 1891, and the estate originally included 500 acres of land. In 1899, the mansion had to be rebuilt because of a kitchen fire. Mary had her own church on the property which was never rebuilt after catching on fire.

Mary Hayes was the cousin of President Rutherford B. Hayes. She was a very spiritual woman and her guests included Sarah Winchester. There were some people who believed that Mary Hayes had healing powers. Mary died four months before she was going to move into the mansion.

Mary had two sons: Everis Anson and Jay Orley. They had a fortune from iron stock, but during the stock market crash, they ran low on money and moved back east. For fifty years, the sprawling estate was abandoned and subject to trespassers, including ghost hunters. Then in the '80s, restoration on the mansion began, and it was reopened for business. The Hayes Mansion has been magnificently restored. Weddings and conferences are held there, and there is a bar and rooms available for overnight guests.

The first employee who shared information with me was Mary A. She was walking out to her car when I interviewed her in the parking lot.

Dottie's Pond, arguably haunted by the ghost of Dottie.

The Haunted Hayes Mansion.

Employees have witnessed plenty of paranormal activity.

According to Mary, the accounting office door slams on its own. Mary mentioned an encounter a guest had which caused the frightened guest to check out early.

In 2003, a married couple were spending the night inside of the mansion's Laurel suite. The husband and wife went down stairs to the bar for a drink. The lady went back to the Laurel suite by herself when she was ready to go to bed. As the woman was trying to sleep, she heard the voices of children playing in the hallway. When she telephoned the lobby to complain about the noise the children were making, the staff insisted there were no children inside the Mansion.

The lady fell asleep for a few minutes, but she was awakened by someone tugging on her blanket. She opened her eyes and saw the ghost of one child tugging on her blanket while the ghost of another child was jumping up and down on her bed. Horrified, she immediately ran out the door of her room while she was still wearing her pajamas. She did not stop running until she made it outside to the curb on the street. She waited at the curb for her husband to bring the car by, so he could pick her up and take her home.

Abbey was bartending when I entered the mansion to hunt down friendly employees for ghost stories. Abbey insisted the ghosts are friendly, too. He's seen shadows and heard doors slamming on their own.

The Hayes Mansion tower is kept under lock and key because the copper that was used for the tower is valuable. They don't want to find anything missing—or they don't want anybody up there because the tower is haunted by a ghost. Only security guards are permitted to enter the tower. Three guests, however, noticed a lady standing in the tower and she was wearing a white gown. The three guests approached the staff and asked about the lady they saw. The staff insisted there was no way for a lady to gain access to the tower because it was constantly locked. The lady in the white gown was a ghost.

A couple of girls who worked on the night shift at the Hayes Mansion quit after working only two months or less. One of them was afraid to go to the restroom alone, and during her shift at the Hayes Mansion, she heard disembodied voices behind her. I next spoke with a restaurant hostess by the name of Briana. She has witnessed the restaurant door opening and closing by itself and has heard the sound of children running upstairs when there weren't any children on the property.

The basement is referred to as "the dungeon." Employees are scared to go down into the basement of the mansion. It has its share of ghost activity.

An employee by the name of Bill went down to the creepy basement and he heard voices coming from the maintenance room. He wanted to scare those people he heard inside. As he was approaching the room, he held onto his keys so the sound of them jingling would not be heard by

the people he thought were inside the room. The voices became louder when Bill quietly inserted his key into the door lock. Bill turned the key and opened the door. But all of a sudden, the voices he heard became silent. To Bill's surprise, the lights inside of the maintenance room were turned off and there was nobody inside the room.

Ashur P. was the last employee I interviewed at the Hayes Mansion. He provided most of the information I received, in addition to taking me on a brief guided tour of the second floor. One evening, Josh, an assistant manager at the mansion, and Ashur were on a tour in the dark. They were inside the Santa Theresa Room and Josh was calling out the name: Mary Hayes. The curtains moved around, even though the window was closed. Josh called Mary's name again, and all of a sudden, they heard the sound of knocking coming from inside the closet. There were several people inside the room, and Josh and Arthur thought someone in the room with them knocked on the closet. People were laughing. But when Josh looked out the window again, he noticed a baby's footprint on the window that was not there one minute earlier. They did not attempt to rub the print off and Ashur wonders if the print is still on the window. The door of that particular room was locked.

Ashur and a co-worker went down a staircase that he showed to me. At the bottom of the staircase is a room on the right-hand side. They tried to open the door of the room, but they were unable to do so. They walked across the hall to where an elevator was located. They were about to take the elevator down to the first floor when suddenly, they heard a screeching noise and the door they could not open was now ajar.

An employee was vacuuming the restaurant inside of the Hayes Mansion. As they were vacuuming the carpet, they were startled to see the ghost of an old lady standing in the middle of a table. The ghost's body was coming through the wooden table top. The employee ended up putting in two weeks notice.

So why not stop by and take a tour of the Hayes Mansion—you don't even need two weeks notice.

Chapter Ten:
GHOSTS SOUTH OF SAN JOSE

THE CASA GRANDE
ALMADEN ROAD

The Casa Grande, on Almaden Road, was originally the mining headquarters for the quicksilver mines inside the mountain across the street. And I remember sneaking into one of the mines (with a friend) years ago. Construction on The Casa Grande began in 1850 and was completed in 1854. There are rumors that The Casa Grande used to be a brothel and a place where bootleggers operated during prohibition. In 1920, The Opry House, which was part of the same building The Casa Grande occupies, was opened for business. An outdoor dance pavilion existed before The Opry House became a theatre. Club Almaden was located behind The Opry House, and the resort included a swimming pool and a restaurant. Club Almaden folded in the 70s, but The Opry House survived until the lease expired, in 1999. In 1997, The County took over the property and construction on The Casa Grande mining museum began.

Terri Sanisio is the Park Interpreter at The Casa Grande, which is the mining museum that opened in 1999.

Teri has worked at the museum for more than five years and she said, "Rangers will not go into the kitchen downstairs and the help do not want to be down there at night." The poltergeist down there is unhappy and he has thrown salt shakers across the kitchen. The ghost is a man who owned a restaurant where the catering company exists. Unfortunately, the restaurant went out of business and he went out back and shot himself in the head. He is most likely the miserable ghost who threw the salt and pepper shakers.

Apparently, nothing seems to discourage me from investigating a haunted place, including an angry poltergeist. I asked Terri if I could see the downstairs kitchen. Unfortunately, it was off limits because the county was renting it to a catering business. But I tried...

In April of 2000, Terri was using the restroom at the museum and there was nobody there except her. As Teri was powdering her nose, she heard ten footsteps and the sound of the upstairs door slowly opening and closing. Terri thought it was either Lisa or a stranger who'd just walked upstairs. Less than one minute later, Terri rushed out of the restroom to see who was there. When Terri reached the top of the stairs and tried to open the door to the room, she was surprised to find the door was locked. And there was nobody inside the room or downstairs.

The haunted Casa Grande.
At least two different ghosts have been sighted on the property.

One morning, a volunteer computer operator came down the stairs at eight-thirty a.m. She asked Terri if the place was haunted because she heard some unexplainable footsteps coming up the stairs. In 2003, a girl was working on the computer and she suddenly felt a cold draft which blew the door open. She called out to see if any one was downstairs, but there was no reply. She walked out to the foyer and went down a few stairs. When she turned the corner of the staircase, she clearly saw the reddish top of a ghost's head. The ghost of a man had one arm on the hand rail as he was descending the stairs. The employee was not afraid of the ghost and was quite comfortable with the encounter.

On Sunday June 6, 2004, we returned to The Casa Grande and I purchased Michael Boulland's book. Before I said a word, Terri recognized me and said, "I haven't seen or heard about anything lately. I told Christina Randall that she is welcome and we are happy to have her on the property."

I said, "Wait a minute. What is going on?"

Terri replied, "Well, they suspect that Christiana Randall is the ghost who's been sighted on the premises. She was the wife of a mine manager. Christiana Randall was a Methodist who had six children and her hair was red."

Another woman, who was a prostitute, is also on the suspect list of ghosts haunting the museum. The Pope family lived on the property in the 60s. People have seen the ghost of a woman looking out of an upstairs window of The Casa Grande.

During the summer of 2007, I met with Terri again and she helped make this book possible. A man and his daughter, who visit the museum, claim the Randall Room is haunted. The ghost is "on a loop" and her name is Jennifer. She is twelve years old, wearing a blue dress, and has long red hair. As the man and his daughter stood inside of the Randall Room, they saw the ghost of Jennifer standing at the doorway. She looked into the room and she was giggling.

Every time I visit the museum, I walk into the Randall Room and it basically gives me the creeps. A small group of church ladies, who made a hobby out of cleansing haunted places, went to The Casa Grande and they tried to get rid of the ghost or ghosts that haunt the museum. They had a prayer circle and Terri has not noticed anything unusual since the ladies were there. I'm under the impression that there is probably a ghost who still remains on the property.

THE ENTIRE BLOCK IS HAUNTED
ALMADEN ROAD

Less than one mile down the road from The Casa Grande lives Tim P. He lives inside an old house and the place is probably haunted. His ex-girlfriend informed me about Tim hearing footsteps in the middle of the night. Tim walked out into his living room and asked: "Who's there?" But there was no one there. Tim's ex-wife thought the place might be haunted, too.

Next door to Tim's property is a house that used to be a jail and the place is haunted—perhaps by souls who were inmates at the jail.

Ron is a friend of Tim's who said, "Tim's entire block is haunted.

HAUNTED HICKS ROAD

Hicks Road has earned a reputation for being haunted. More than one person was hit and killed by a car while riding their bicycles along the road. And at least one bicycling ghost has been sighted by witnesses driving there.

I've heard a story about a guy who was driving under the influence on Hicks Road. His girlfriend was in the car with him and he lost control of the vehicle and wrecked. She was killed in the accident, but he lived. Six months later, he was driving under the influence again on Hicks Road, and others were in the car with him. The ghost of his girlfriend appeared on the road and caused him to have an accident. He was the only person who died in this wreck.

The ghost punished her boyfriend, taking his life the same way she lost hers—because he was driving under the influence.

THE CHART HOUSE
IN LOS GATOS

South of San Jose is the upscale town of Los Gatos. Most of the ghosts in Los Gatos seem to be located on North Santa Cruz Avenue. Trevise, formerly The Chart House, is a restaurant located on North Santa Cruz. Trevise is an old Victorian home with a lovely outdoor patio in front of the restaurant. An orthopedic therapist at The Santa Theresa Kaiser, by the name of Janet, told me about a ghost existing at the restaurant when it was called The Chart House.

The building, originally the Cogschall Mansion, was erected in 1891 and served as a household before becoming a funeral parlor, years later. Jeff was bartending at the Chart House when I visited the restaurant, a few years ago. He was from San Diego and had worked at the restaurant for one year. First, let me say that Jeff did not give his cell phone number to any of the employees who worked at the Chart House. Sometimes when Jeff was downstairs, his cell phone rang, but nobody was on the other line. And Jeff's caller ID revealed that he was receiving these particular calls from the telephone in the restaurant upstairs. Others were in the restaurant at the time Jeff received the phone calls, but no one was on the upstairs phone calling Jeff.

Jeff also heard the sound of light footsteps coming from the second-story dining section of the restaurant. He was absolutely the only person inside the restaurant. Late one evening, a dishwasher, who used to work there, saw the ghost of a young girl walking inside the vacant restaurant. The ghost is probably the five-year-old daughter of the property's original owners.

It was late in the evening and a restaurant manager locked up the Chart House to walk down the street to make a bank deposit. When he arrived back at the eating establishment, he was surprised to find all of the candles inside the restaurant were lit; and the restaurant was still locked up.

Jeff showed me two large champagne bottles that were on display inside the dining room. One day, he noticed the bottles were turned around and both labels were facing the wall. Jeff assumed a member of the staff was cleaning and they were responsible for the label on the bottles facing backwards. Jeff turned both of the large bottles around so the labels were facing out and walked away for a few minutes. When he entered the dining room a few minutes later, he was shocked to notice both of the bottles had been turned around again, and both labels were not visible. There were no other employees inside the restaurant at the time.

Additionally, witnesses have seen the ghost in the cupola, as they were walking in front of the restaurant.

Stephanie works at Trevise and she told me about Scott's experiences. Scott is a cook at the restaurant and he has witnessed some of the paranormal activity which has occurred there. While he was alone working in the kitchen, a cart was pushed towards him by an invisible force.

In the kitchen, there are a bunch of plates stacked on a shelf. Scott was the only employee on the premises. He went into another room for a minute. When he walked back into the kitchen, he was surprised to find all of the plates had moved and were now stacked on top of a nearby table.

Because the restaurant was once a funeral parlor, I wonder if there is more than one ghost haunting the premises—and maybe whether they're looking for their last meal...

THE LAST CALL
NORTH SANTA CRUZ AVENUE

I journeyed into a bar called The 49er to see if they had any ghosts. The lady who was bartending did not think The 49er was haunted, but she told me about a ghost I'll call the Jager ghost. On North Santa Cruz Avenue, in the Los Gatos Shopping Center, was a bar called The Last Call. The bar had a customer who loved Jagermeister. One day, he ended up dying inside the bar because he drank too much.

His ghost was known to hang out next to the Jagermeister dispenser and most of the paranormal activity took place near it. Sometimes people were missing their keys after placing them down near the dispenser.

Unfortunately, The Last Call was closed and the building is now empty. But the Jager ghost probably continues to linger on the property which will eventually be occupied by a business in the future. And that business might end up being haunted by the Jager ghost. (Only next time, maybe a water cooler will be his venue...)

THE CATS
HIGHWAY 17

More than one person I know suggested: The Cats in Los Gatos is haunted. The restaurant is located on Highway 17 between Los Gatos and Lexington Reservoir. When I asked a guy at the restaurant about the place having a ghost, he acted skeptical. "Perhaps people hear noises because the building is old," he said. But hear noises they do, and some truly believe that there's some haunting going on. I've been in the restaurant several times and I would not be surprised if there wasn't a ghost right there with me. There's a feeling...

DARDANELLI LANE

David Derr, along with two roommates, lived in a haunted duplex on Dardanelli Lane, near Los Gatos Community Hospital. According to David, a knife on a kitchen stove top was moving by itself. The front door also locked by itself and the two cats that lived in the duplex acted funny

Trevise is haunted by a child seen in the cupola.

at times. David noticed a faint cloud of energy above him when he was resting in his room.

One day, while David and Brett were next door, their roommate (Julie) was alone in their duplex and she was laying on the bed inside her bedroom. When David arrived back at their duplex, Julie was crying and hysterical. She'd felt a ghost poking her—and the ghost was being rough. David had come back because he knew something was wrong. He ended up moving next door with the neighbors. There were no problems at *their* duplex.

LOS GATOS COMMUNITY HOSPITAL

I saw a picture of a deserted nursing station at Los Gatos Community Hospital. Standing at the station was the ghost of a nurse in a white uniform. Only the lower half of her body appeared in the photograph. The nurse appears to be working at the station and not lingering around the area. She probably worked in that unit, years ago. Institutions are notoriously haunted by ex-employees who may not know they are dead—and they still show up for work.

GREEN VALLEY DISPOSAL COMPANY

Green Valley was located at 644 North Santa Cruz Avenue. There were stories about the company having a ghost in the building they occupied. Office furniture moved around and strange noises were heard. The disposal company no longer exists at that address on the Avenue. The ghosts that haunted the company possibly lived on the property or nearby, years ago.

GHOSTS AT BRIAN'S HOUSE
MORE LOS GATOS

Brian Glenn was born in Los Gatos. During the last Christmas at his father's house, Brian was taking care of his dying father. Crystal is Brian's daughter, and when she was under the Christmas tree, she saw the ghost of Brian's mom. Crystal never met her grandmother, but she accurately described her wearing pink slippers.

After Brian's father passed away, every night for a while, Brian heard the door leading to the garage opening and closing. Brian climbed out of bed to make sure a burglar was not in the house, but there was never a burglar in the house or in the garage.

One night, Brian was sleeping in his parents' room after they'd passed away. At three a.m., he had to get out of that room because he felt a weird vibe that was scaring him. Brian probably felt this way because the ghost of his parents may have been present—after all, it had been their bedroom.

Brian painted the house blue with a white trim and sold it to a lady who painted the house an army green color. When Brian's dad lived in the house, it was painted the same shade of green. Was Brian's father still around to influence yet another family?

TWO PEOPLE SAW THE GHOST
NORTH SANTA CRUZ AVENUE

According to Bill Wulf, the Los Gatos Cemetery existed where Double D's Sport Bar is located on North Santa Cruz Avenue. The cemetery extended down to where Pedro's Mexican Restaurant was built. Bill thinks the bodies were left in the ground, and numerous businesses were built on top of the cemetery. One of these businesses is The Beu Chevoux hair salon.

I was hoping not to interrupt a customer's hair cut when I dropped by the salon. But that's what happened, so I tried not to wear out my welcome. Heidi was cutting a lady's hair when I walked through the door. (After the lady heard us talking about the place being haunted, she had a semi-horrified look on her face!)

Jean is the owner of The Beu Chevoux and she, along with a guy who worked next door to the salon, encountered the ghost of a man in the salon. Jean and the guy next door were frightened by the encounter and they both stayed outside for a little while.

The ghost may originate from the cemetery beneath the salon. It's hard to substantiate who some ghosts are and where they come from. But a business on top of a cemetery is a good clue.

THE LOS GATOS OPERA HOUSE

Built in 1904, the Opera House is a historic landmark located at 140 West Main Street, and mostly, weddings are held there. A guy was taking a picture of the opera house and the ghost of a woman appeared in the photograph. She is standing behind one of the upstairs windows. An employee, by the name of Trisha, gave to me a copy of the ghost photo. The interior of the Opera House has been magnificently restored, and when I'm upstairs on the second floor, I have the impression and opinion that the place is haunted.

Musicians performing at wedding receptions have witnessed some of the paranormal activity, including their instruments being moved. I'm unaware of any sightings that have taken place at The Opera House, but the ghosts have shown up in pictures. Trisha was photographed inside the building. The dark silhouette of a ghost appeared in the picture, standing on the second level behind her. The picture of Trisha and the ghost was printed in a local newspaper. The ghosts might be former employees of the Opera House or former patrons who enjoyed the entertainment they were present for at the facility years ago.

The Los Gatos Opera House. Ghosts appeared for pictures.

A Traumatic Encounter at Los Gatos High School

A student who attended Los Gatos High School jumped out of a second story window of the business building and fell to his death. His ghost haunts the high school and he has appeared for students. In 1991, a football player went to his locker and the ghost of the student appeared. The football player flipped out and needed psychiatric help after encountering the student ghost.

Thirty Three Ghosts Were Sighted Wright's Station Tunnel

I have no idea if Wright's Station Tunnel is still haunted. According to Barbara Smith's book, "33 ghosts were seen by a man who was passing by the tunnel on a horse carriage, in 1890. It was a stormy night and his horse team froze as he was passing the tunnel. He looked at the tunnel and saw the ghosts of thirty-three workers, who were killed by a natural gas explosion, emerging from the tunnel, then vanishing. Many others who were at the tunnel at midnight have seen the ghosts walking out of the tunnel." (Smith, 2000, 98)

I have not been at Wright's Station tunnel at midnight. But I have visited the tunnel and people can walk into its depths for about a quarter of a mile. The majority of the tunnel has been blocked off with big piles of dirt.

Construction on the tunnel began in 1877 and was finished in 1880. The station was torn down in 1936 because The San Jose Water Company purchased the land. The railroad operated north of the station, from Alma to Los Gatos, until 1940. Part of the railroad track is still visible today. The water company owns the tunnel and patrols it, but I have never seen anybody getting kicked out by the water company. Off Summit Road is Merrill Road, which leads to Wright's Station Road. The tunnel is on the left hand side of the road, before the bridge.

Beware the time, though, least you find yourself among a crowd of thirty-three...

GHOSTS OF MORGAN HILL
PEEBLES DRIVE

South of San Jose is the town of Morgan Hill. John Viray lived in a Victorian home on Peebles Drive. Sometimes John was afraid to go into the house alone, so he would wait for his sister or brother-in-law to arrive home. One day, John's brother-in-law, Anthony, saw a ghost sitting on the porch as he was pulling up in his car. When Anthony opened his car door and stepped out of the car, the ghost was gone. Anthony was ready to challenge the ghost and protect his home.

Anthony's son, Mathew, began seeing the ghost of a man wearing a black sweater. Mathew told his parents about the ghost, but there was not much they could do about it. Yet, Mathew was stressed out everyday because of the ghost. They took him to a doctor because he had developed bald spots from the stress the ghost was causing him. Thankfully, his hair eventually grew back.

When John moved into the house, the light in the garage burned out and did not work again until they were moving out. And they had no choice but to move out of that house—that's how fear works.

Is it possible that a person who used to own the house might be residing there as a ghost. Maybe the ghost feels that the family members are the trespassers in this situation...

A HAUNTED RESTAURANT
NEAR HIGHWAY 101 AND COCHRANE ROAD

John V. was eating at El Capri, near Highway 101 and Cochrane Road when he heard that the restaurant's basement was haunted by the ghost of a man who was killed by his son. They were fighting in the basement and the son shot his father. Witnesses have seen the ghost in the basement, and they hear noises down there. An employee offered to show John the basement—but he declined.

A PARANOID LADY IN MORGAN HILL

Wendy, who worked at the Gas Lighter Theatre, knew of a lady in Morgan Hill whose daughter passed away. The daughter was haunting the property. The lady boarded up her daughter's bedroom, boarded up the fireplace, and placed mirrors around the living room. This lady went through a lot of trouble to keep tabs on the ghost of her daughter. It may be that she is over reacting as a result of paranoia. Or is she?

OUIJA BOARD IN THE FIREPLACE

Wendy also knew about a girl in Morgan Hill who was using a Ouija board by herself. The girl's mom was ironing clothes and the television was on. The girl left the pointer on the Ouija board, and that is never a good idea. The pointer began moving on its own. The girl's father became angry and he broke the Ouija board into four pieces. And as he, one by one, tossed the pieces into the burning fire place, a disembodied scream was heard in the room.

Burning a Ouija board is not a good idea because a ghost might become violently upset about the communication ending. And then you never know what might happen...

A HAUNTED HIGHWAY—
HIGHWAY 152 WEST

The Mt. Madonna Inn is on Highway 152 West and I stopped by to find out if they had any ghost stories. An employee did not have stories about the Inn, but he told me about the headless ghost of a motorcycle rider who has been sighted on Highway 152 West. Most likely, the motorcycle rider was killed on the road in that area. Maybe he was decapitated or his head is not appearing for those who see the ghost of him and his motorcycle.

HAUNTED RUINS
MT. MADONNA PARK

Mt. Madonna Park is reportedly haunted by a Henry Miller and his daughter, who fell to her death, as she was riding a horse. The foundation of Miller's mansion is still intact. We explored the remains of the mansion and did not see any ghosts, but there are people that have.

A HAUNTED AMUSEMENT PARK
GILROY GARDENS

Gilroy Gardens on Highway 152 West is haunted. Guests and employees have witnessed paranormal activity at the park, including lights acting up and the carousel operating by itself. The amusement park, formerly known as Bonfonte Gardens, is located in a town which has earned a reputation for having its share of ghosts.

A Ghost Combing Its Hair
Gilroy

Mary Romesberg lives in Gilroy, and while she was looking in the bathroom mirror, she noticed the ghost of a guy combing his hair. Mary was startled and her commotion caused the ghost to react. It changed to a shapeless cloud of energy and went up into the corner of the room. Mary was unable to move for a moment. Then everything was fine. She asked me if I knew that ghosts could change their shape (which I did).

The house behind Mary's is also haunted and the ghosts involved might be a Japanese couple who lived there. Mary, her boyfriend, Eric, and his friend were remodeling the house behind Mary's—that is how they found out the house was haunted. Apparently, there are several ghosts there, both male and female. The spirits have been to Mary's house, too, and she thinks they were in the yard and the trees of the backyard behind hers. The ghosts tried to hide from Mary after she saw them.

One of the ghosts resembles Eric. The first time Mary saw him was years ago. One night, she was returning home from work and when she pulled up in her car, the ghost was standing outside her house. Mary assumed it was Eric waiting for her. But when she went inside and confronted Eric, she found out it was not he who was waiting for her at all, so late in the evening. It was a ghost standing outside her house.

One night, Mary left the key in her bedroom door lock for Eric. Hours later, she noticed that the bedroom door was slightly ajar and Marie saw a ghost's hand slowly trying to turn the key. In an authoritative voice, Mary told the ghost, "Please leave." The ghost complied.

Still another time, Mary was leaving for work. When she closed her front door, she did not notice her dog, Gretchen, had been left outside the house. As Mary was walking towards her car, the ghost yelled, "Hey!" Mary stopped and went back to see what was going on. It was then that she realized Gretchen was outside and that the ghost was bringing this to her attention.

Mary mostly sees the ghosts at night, and Eric's friend actually spoke with the ghosts on one occasion. The spirits asked Eric's friend what he was doing, and Eric explained he was doing construction work and remodeling the house. Then the ghosts began playing games with Mary by imitating the sound of people working on the house behind hers.

Sometimes Mary will get scared. She was cleaning her neighbor's house late one evening when she heard noises approaching her. A female voice said, "Hey!" and the ghost's tone of voice was not very pleasant. It forced Mary to finally yell, "Please back off!" And the ghost obliged.

But there were pleasant experiences, also. Mary had her boom box with her and a tune was playing on the radio. Mary heard voices singing the Star Spangled Banner in the background. She joined in and was singing along with the ghosts. The tune became more and more beautiful and had a lovely ending.

A New Haunted House in Gilroy

Marty, who works for the county, bought a new house in Gilroy. The reason the house is haunted may be because a school or other structure existed on the property and was torn down. Some of the issues that gives Marty reason to believe this is that his television acts abnormally and two new video game systems are problematic. One of the systems already broke down. A door that rubs against a thick carpet closed by itself, too.

They suspect the ghost of a man wearing a red flannel shirt maybe haunting the property.

The Ghost of Emmett

My brother, Richard, and his girlfriend, Sandra, live at her house in Gilroy. Sometimes, a ghost comes by to visit them and several things have happened. They've heard the front screen door opening and closing, but when Sandra's daughter looked, no one was there. Sandra's sister was living with them for a little while, and sometimes, she was missing a dress. Eventually, it would show back up. A box fell off a shelf and there was not a natural explanation, according to Richard. He and Sandra were in the bedroom with the door ajar and they heard the steps of a ghost coming down the stairs. Out of the corner of their eyes, they saw a silhouette at the bottom of the staircase. A child who was in the upstairs bathroom said there was a ghost there.

The ghost who visits them comes and goes and is a harmless prankster. They came up with Emmett as a nick name for the ghost.

Chapter Eleven:

GHOSTS WEST OF SAN JOSE

BR&F SPRAY—
SANTA CLARA

Charlene Rubino told me about BR&F Spray in Santa Clara being haunted. She was under the impression that the ghosts at BR&F were unfriendly because they are the restless souls of victims who were killed by an evil boss.

Brian and the ladies working in the office welcomed me. They were unfamiliar with Charlene's theory about the ghosts, but they did have ghost stories to share with me. The original owner of the company built the business on land which used to be an orchard. One fellow thinks the business was built on top of an Indian burial ground, which are throughout Santa Clara. (And that's never a good thing.)

One day, Charlene's ex-brother-in-law was working at BR&F Spray. A lady, who was wearing a low-cut dress, was walking by him. He stepped aside to get out of her way as she continued walking into the building—only he

Employees have encountered ghosts at the BR&F Spray company.

noticed that the lady never came back out of the building. She must have been a ghost because she was not inside the building, and there was no other way out of the building.

When people know they are speaking with a ghost on the telephone, the conversation is usually brief. One evening, Brian noticed the top light on his telephone blinking, but the phone was not ringing—and it should have been. Brian picked up the receiver and heard the ghost of a young boy crying for help. He's never ended a telephone conversation so quickly before!

More than one sighting has occurred at the company. Barbara was working in an office there, and as she stood up and walked down a hallway, she glanced into a room. She saw a person was standing next to her father. Barbara assumed it was her son, especially since the person had a husky build like her son. But Barbara ran into her son a moment later in a different section of the company. The figure she saw standing near her father must have been a ghost. The figure she observed had vanished from the premises.

Late one evening, Brian and Dennis were closing the business. Dennis was walking through the warehouse and a malevolent ghost pushed a cart into him. The cart smacked him in the head.

Robert W. is a 300-pound Army Ranger who had a reputation for being a bad dude. One night, Brian and Robert were closing the warehouse and they both heard a child's eerie scream coming from behind a booth. Robert W. ran out of there as fast as a marathon winner.

Barbara suggested the ghosts might be patients who were locked up in Agnew's State Hospital, which is not far away from BR&F Spray. Of course, anything is possible in the ghost world...

THE GHOST OF AN UNCLE— SANTA CLARA

Charlene Rubino's Aunt's house in Santa Clara is haunted. Her uncle died at the hospital, but he still roams the halls of her Aunt's house. Charlene heard ghostly footsteps walking down the hall, late at night, and she could hear the sound of change jingling in her uncle's pocket, as his ghost walked down the hallway.

A HAUNTED UNIVERSITY— SANTA CLARA

Santa Clara University has earned a reputation for being haunted, but when I questioned some of the students and faculty members about the O'Connor building being haunted or the church tower having ghosts, there was not a lot of information offered. There's reportedly ghostly activity, but no one was willing to fess up to the details. Of course, not every student on campus is aware of the ghost stories. Some students are new and may not hear a story until they've reached their junior year. From what I've heard, though, ghosts of monks are sighted in the tower. The mission existed on the property the school occupies. Students and staff have heard doors to buildings closing, when no one was near the doors of the O'Connor building.

Added to that, the college is located near a cemetery.

Could it be that those at the campus are spooked by the controversy? Or is it merely discomfort billowing from the nearby cemetery? Education, after all can be harrowing...

A HAUNTED GROCERY STORE— SANTA CLARA

Safeway is across the street from Santa Clara University. Greg W. and Julie M. were shopping at 12:30 am when they heard a crashing sound. They walked over to the flower section as a store employee was approaching the area. A large red vase inexplicably fell on the ground.

"There's another story for David Lee," Julie said.

A HAUNTED INSANE ASYLUM— SANTA CLARA

Sun Micro Systems now occupies the property where Agnews once stood. Naturally, they inherited ghosts from Agnews. A new campus was constructed and the buildings that remain from Agnews are mostly used for conferences. Christina Ruiz works for Sun Micro Systems. She showed me around the auditorium in addition to giving me a tour of the mansion where the administrator for Agnews resided. As Christina and I walked through the mansion, I felt as if I was walking through a haunted house.

Agnews was constructed in 1889, and at one point in time, the patient population reached 10,000. During the 1906 earthquake, Agnews lost more lives than the city of San Francisco. Patients were running loose and had to be tied to telephone poles and fire hydrants. Agnews even had their own graveyard which was located up the street from the property.

Some of the souls who suffered at the hospital now haunt the property and continue to be miserable. Employees who worked at Agnews saw ghosts and they heard disembodied voices and screaming. One of the ghost encounters that took place at Sun Micro Systems was reported to me by Christina Ruiz. Three phone technicians were working in the dark inside one of the buildings. Two men and a woman encountered the ghost of a girl inside of a closet. The two men had flashlights, but the woman did not. The lady opened the closet and saw the ghost of a girl with her arms open, as if she wanted someone to take her with them. The lady jumped back, terrified. The other two saw the ghost and all three of them started running as fast as they could. The lady was not as fast as the men were. She was trying her best to catch up with them while screaming for them to wait for her.

GHOSTS NEAR LAFAYETTE STREET

Doug Grigsby lives in Santa Clara near Lafayette Street. When Doug's father was dying, his mom saw the spirits of relatives floating in the air above him. They were there to welcome him the moment he passed away. After he died, Doug began hearing strange noises around the house. After his mom passed away, he witnessed a door in front of him closing. Doug also heard the sound of water as if the washing machine was operating. In his mom's bathroom, he found the toilet paper unrolled and on the floor. Doug is convinced his mom is now watching over him in spirit.

Another short story comes from Nancy L. who was babysitting in Santa Clara, years ago. While she was reading next to a lamp, she saw the head of a ghost, but not the body. The ghost was a man and Nancy was not frightened of the ghost. He disappeared a moment later.

A GHOST FLYING IN THE AIR
DUANE AVENUE

Formerly located on Duane Avenue in Santa Clara was Potpouri. Jose Diaz worked in the warehouse at Potpouri between 1994 and 1998. A friend, who grew up with him, passed away and the next day, Jose returned to the warehouse with a few beers. He and his co-workers were hanging out and having a discussion about his now-deceased friend. A while later, a couple of beer cans sitting on a table began moving forward by themselves. The cans were swinging from side to side as they made their way forward. This normally should not have occurred especially because the table had a flat surface.

One of Jose's co-workers had taken a picture inside the Potpouri warehouse and a flying ghost appeared in the picture. When the employee told Jose and other employees about the photo, they did not believe him until he brought the picture to work and showed it to them. According to Jose, in the picture, there is indeed a ghost flying through the air in the warehouse. The ghost's fingers were visible, and they resembled bones. It did have a solid appearance.

PARAMOUNT'S GREAT AMERICA

Formerly Marriott's Great America, Paramount's Great America is haunted, and most of the ghosts seem to be victims who died on different rides at the amusement park. The first deaths at the park occurred not long after it first opened. A roller coaster, called the Turn of the Century, was the site of the park's most tragic accident. Two corkscrews (the loops on the coaster's track) existed and the roller coaster car fell off the track while it was upside down. A number of people died as a result of the tragedy.

The park's second death occurred on a roller coaster called Willard's Wizard. A guest, who was riding in the very last seat of the car, got bumped by an incoming car. He fell back onto the track and was run over by the incoming car. (My brother and his ex-girlfriend were at the base of the ride when the tragedy occurred.)

Frank Teliao was my co-worker at O'Connor Hospital and he used to work at Great America. One evening, Frank and his co-worker were standing near the park's front entrance and both of them heard the cries of a child. They searched the area, but there was no child to be found.

Two employees, who worked at the Top Gun roller coaster as ride operators, were closing the ride one night. They were shocked to encounter a person standing near them, whose head they could not see. The person was obviously a ghost. The employees were traumatized by the incident and they transferred to a different work area. Either, the ghost was a person who was decapitated, it chose to not show its head, or the atmosphere replayed the ghost without the head appearing.

I remember when a kid died on the Drop Zone Stunt Tower because he was not properly strapped in—he haunts the tower now. Another guest was killed because he jumped a fence to retrieve his hat. The roller coaster came by and a foot, belonging to a girl on the ride, hit him in the head—and he died. Is the premises of the coaster now haunted by the hat chaser?

It is said that not only the Drop Zone Stunt Tower is haunted, but also the nearby arcade where the ghost of a man, seen by security on their surveillance camera monitor, visits to possibly watch over a game or two. Additionally, both the Imax Theatre and the Paramount Theatre have their own haunts—acting out perhaps? And I shouldn't forget the Roast Beef Shop where a ghostly man screams from inside a locked freezer.

A HAUNTED CAFETERIA
WEB EX

For a year and a half, John Viray worked at Guckenheimer Catering Company. John helped out at the cafeteria at Web Ex, which is near Great America and heard from Renzie, another employee, about a ghostly lady in the cafeteria. The ghost appears in the corner of the cafeteria, and walks back and forth, appearing early in the morning.

ENDLESS GHOST STORIES
AT BROOKDALE LODGE

Brookdale Lodge is around twenty-five miles South East of San Jose. The lodge is on Highway 9 in the town of Brookdale, between Boulder Creek and Felton. The lodge was built in 1923, and movie stars, including Marilyn Monroe, have stayed there.

In 1999, I spent the night at Brookdale Lodge and went hunting for ghosts with my video camera. The friendly employees handed me the keys to the most haunted rooms on the property. I went into room number 31 and 32 to take pictures. I also interviewed the owner's daughter, who saw the ghost of a girl who drowned in the river that runs through the restaurant. The ghost was sitting on a circular-shaped chair in the lobby, and was gone when she returned to the area.

I talked with a waiter at the lodge who brought me back to the kitchen to show me an area where a ghost was making a lot of noise, but nothing was ever disturbed. Then I heard a wild story from Kim at the lodge. She told me a wild story. She and a friend were given a ride by a guy who was driving a pickup truck. They climbed inside his truck and drove down the road. She said to her friend, "He is not real. And neither is this truck." Of course her friend did not believe her. But after they dropped the friend off and continued down the road, the truck stopped again and they both stepped out. The truck disappeared and the guy flew into an old shack. She joined him in the shack and made love to him. (A ghostly rendezvous? This is the most hard-core story I've ever heard at the lodge.)

But there are more short snippet stories of the Brookdale Lodge.

One day, the jukebox at the lodge was playing a song. Perhaps the ghost did not like the song that was playing because the jukebox cracked and broke, though no one was standing next to it.

I recently heard about a room at the lodge that is unavailable for guests because it is too haunted.

Chelsea A. was spending the night at the lodge with a friend. Chelsea saw the ghost of a man wearing a top hat. When she looked again, he'd already disappeared.

A couple of guys were at the lodge calling the name of Sarah. Sarah is supposed to be the name of the girl drowned in the river running through the lodge's restaurant. As the guys were driving away from the lodge, their car lights continued flashing on and off and would not stop until they turned around and drove back to the lodge. The ghost had followed them out of the lodge.

There are rumors that the mob whacked a double-crosser and buried the body somewhere on the grounds of the lodge.

Brookdale Lodge hosts musical guests, and sometimes a pretty big name shows up, including Pete Best, original drummer for The Beatles. The Tubes rock-and-roll band performed there, too. Fee Waybil, the lead singer, asked the crowd if the lodge was haunted. "Yes," the crowd yelled back. (It seems to be common knowledge.)

Some people believe the lodge has a lot of ghosts. Roger is an employee who has been working at the lodge for a while. He told me stories I've never heard before. According to witnesses, toilet paper rolls were spinning on their own in numerous rooms at the same time. In the lodge's bar is a video game, a television, and a jukebox. George Harrison had just died, and they were watching a television announcement stating that George passed away. George's music was playing, during the broadcast. The funny thing was, the song that was playing on the television was also playing on the jukebox. Someone checked the jukebox's song list, and the George Harrison song they were hearing was not one of the selections on the list.

One morning at five-thirty, an employee arrived at the lodge. He was the only person on the property. He went inside and heard big band music. He assumed the stereo was on, but when he checked it, the power was off. There was no sound coming out of the stereo speakers. The employee was terrified and he no longer goes into the lodge unless someone goes inside with him.

One evening, a reggae band was playing in the lodge's ballroom. The band was charging five dollars a person for admittance into the show. Next to the ballroom area was a pool table. A wedding party paid quite a bit of money to have their reception at the lodge and some of the people affiliated with the wedding party were playing pool. The reggae band's management was insisting that the wedding party guests pay five dollars a piece to be in that area. The wedding party felt that they'd already paid to be there, and they had no intention of paying five dollars a piece. The conflict escalated into a shouting match. All of a sudden, the power went out at the lodge for two hours, in Boulder Creek for ten minutes, and in Felton for five minutes. There was still power flowing to the grid, but power was out. The moment the drummer of the reggae band was carrying the last piece of his drum set out the door of the lodge, the power mysteriously turned back on. Evidently, there's a ghost at the lodge who dislikes arguing.

A punk rock band was performing at Brookdale Lodge. Apparently, a ghost did not want to hear the band's music. The band was jamming and the power turned off. Roger checked the fuse box and was surprised to see all of the breakers turned off. Roger had never seen anything like this happen before. After he finished resetting all of the breakers inside the fuse box, the band started playing again. But the power went out again. Roger looked at the fuse box and found all of the breakers turned off again. He had to reset the breakers three times—and the band was out of luck.

A group of paranormal investigators were at Brookdale Lodge, and they brought cameras and other equipment with them. When members of the group were standing next to Roger, their equipment went berserk. One of the investigators took a picture of Roger, and eighteen entities appeared around him in the picture.

Jennifer is a gorgeous bar tender who works at the lodge. The Wave Magazine nominated her for best bartender. One day, Sylvia Brown was in the dining room at Brookdale Lodge. Jennifer walked into the dining room area and she felt a burning sensation on her lips. Sylvia Brown said, "a ghost is kissing you on the lips." Jennifer also mentioned a pinball machine that was playing by itself—it was unplugged at the time.

A Haunted Sporting Goods Store
Sunnyvale

Across the street from Toys R Us in Sunnyvale is Big Five sporting goods store. Big Five was once a grocery store and two kids were playing hide and go seek there. They hid in a freezer and were accidentally locked inside, where they froze to death. That is why the store is haunted.

The second level, in the back of the store, is where most of the paranormal activity occurs. A lady, who works at the store, heard the sound of the ghosts walking across the roof of the building. John B. is an employee, and according to him, moving shadows appear on the surveillance cameras when nobody is inside the store except him and one other employee.

An employee at Century 25 was working there a few years ago. She and others saw objects moving around, felt unexplainable gusts of wind, and roller blades were rolling down the aisle, with no one on them.

During the month of November 2007, John found an Air Soft rifle on the floor. He felt that, most likely, one of the ghosts knocked it down.

As an aside, John also mentioned a creek in Mountain View that's haunted by a boy who was shot in the face. His body was dumped in the creek where the Middlefield Road overpass meets Highway 101. The ghost of the child is mostly sighted at night.

Ghosts of Sunnyvale

Jerry is a county employee who used to live in a haunted house in Sunnyvale. Doors closed on their own and when Jerry was in bed, the sheets were moving—and he was scared. His wife's friend came by to visit, and she noticed the front door was open. She heard voices emerging from the bedroom and figured Jerry and his wife were home. She looked around for them, but they were not home. Nobody was there. The couple, who previously lived in the house, died there. The husband accidentally fell off of the roof to his death. The house was torn down. Is he still around in another form to keep an eye on things?

Bishop Elementary in Sunnyvale is haunted by the ghost of a man.

I heard a rumor about someone going into Toys R Us in Sunnyvale and cleansing the place. The most recent story was from an employee working at the customer service desk. She heard a door slamming near the front left-hand corner of the store when no one was around in the front part of the store where the door is located.

Manuel Barragan knew about a haunted house in Sunnyvale that was torn down. The 911 hotline received a call from the house from Mrs. Brown, who was suffering from a heart attack. When the 911 operator called back to check the status of the situation, the guy staying in the house told them he did not make the call—and he was not having a heart attack. Later, he found an old newspaper in the attic which stated that a woman by the name of Mrs. Brown lived in the house. She'd died of a heart attack there. So she's the one who called 911, years ago.

GHOSTS OF MOUNTAIN VIEW

Pilar P. moved to Mountain View in 1989. When Pilar and her roommate first moved into the property, she found a baby's belongings. The baby clothes gave Pilar a creepy vibe over and over again until she threw them into the trash can. It was then that Pilar and her roommate began hearing the sound of tiny footsteps walking across the living room floor. Activity accelerated to the point where everyone who came over thought they were being followed around by the invisible infant. A psychic happened to be over Pilar's place one day. The psychic asked if someone there had a baby. The answer was no and the psychic became scared because of the ghostly toddler. One night, Pilar woke up and felt as if a baby's skin was rubbing against her arm. Perhaps the ghost was trying to cuddle on her arm. When Pilar moved to her next residence, she did not know if the ghost followed or not. Sometimes, Pilar's child would stare at something and act kind of afraid.

Lisa Fulton was driving near Castro Street in Mountain View. She was arguing with her daughter when the ghost of a girl wearing an old-fashioned dress appeared in front of her car. Lisa had no time to stop and drove right through the ghost. She knew there was no need to turn around and look for a body on the ground. Lisa was so stressed out from arguing with her daughter, the incident did not faze her very much at the time. There is a cemetery in the area where the incident occurred; could a spirit from the grave been looking for a ride?

THE HAUNTED TOWN OF CAMPBELL

Norman Canady lived near Hamilton Avenue and Winchester Boulevard, in Campbell. A ghost has appeared in the back seat of his car. Sometimes, Norman sees the ghost in his rear view mirror, but when he turns around, the ghost is gone. Norman's wife has also seen the ghost and they are not afraid of it, especially since it is always smiling.

Barry B., who works at Century 25, lives in a haunted house in Campbell. His dad came down stairs while everybody was sleeping and found the oven was turned on along with the television. A ghostly snack before the late show perhaps?

Al Mai lived in Campbell with a roommate and it was the first apartment he had ever lived in. One day, Al was resting. He heard his door open and the sound of footsteps walking across the carpet. Al figured his roommate was sneaking up on him, so he pretended to be asleep. When he felt the weight of somebody sitting down on his bed, he quickly turned around to surprise his roommate. But Al was the one who was surprised. There was nobody in his room—except for a ghost he was unable to see. Another time, he was walking in the hallway of his apartment, and something invisible brushed against him. He's also found the volume button on his stereo turned all the way down, over night and he's come home from work to find his own number on his caller id—this happened twice in one week. I told Al, "It's impossible for you to call home from your own house." Al replied, "That's exactly the point." This wasn't the end of ghostly occurrences, however. Al was leaving for work and when he opened his door, he saw a ghost that appeared as a white mist, only visible if he was directly in front of it. The ghost entered Al's place and he, at first, was going to let the ghost stay while he went to work, but he changed his mind and ordered the ghost to leave. No telling what a pesky spirit will do alone in an apartment.

Cathy Zitzer used to live in an apartment in Campbell. Darlene was Cathy's mom, who passed away and Cathy keeps her ashes there. When Cathy brings Darlene's ashes out and places the urn on the table, she sees shadows. After she puts the ashes away, she continues to see shadows for a couple of days; then things return to normal.

Back in the 70s, Cathy and her roommate lived in Campbell, too. The ghost, who haunted the place they lived in, did not like a dog that belonged to Cathy's roommate. The ghost opened the side gate and the front door to let the dog out. Another time, they found the dog was chewing on an electrical cord and they intervened before the dog was electrocuted—this was unusual for this dog to chew on something it was not supposed to. The dog ended up being killed by a car because the side gate was opened.

When Cathy's uncle died for the first time, silhouettes on the other side told him, "Breathe if you want to live." He started breathing and he lived for two more weeks. I spoke with Cathy's brother, Tom, on the telephone. When he died, silhouettes of relatives were welcoming him and he wanted to stay. But fortunately, he sprang back to life and survived a temporary death that included going through the tunnel to the other side.

David Derr's brother, Mitch, and his Fiancé, Christa, lived in an apartment in Campbell, down the street from the Prune Yard. One evening, I was invited to their place and went there after work. There was one candle burning on the table in their apartment and Christa and I were talking about ghosts for about thirty minutes. She mentioned seeing the ghost of her grand father, whose partially-materialized appearance she compared to a fuzzy television screen. Her grandfather was watching over her.

She also mentioned an occasion when she received a phone call from a ghost, who said no words but made an awful growling noise. When Christa mentioned the phone call, Mitch had a funny look on his face and I started laughing. Mitch ended up bringing a digital camera out of his bedroom, and he took a picture of David and I sitting on the couch. Then he went back into the bedroom to develop the photo on his computer. When he brought the picture back into the living room to show it to us, I thought something must have fallen in front of the camera lens. We could see the photograph was ruined by a huge white-trailing streak of energy with rings inside it. At the end was a solid, rounded-off shape aiming at me. Christa said, "It's a ghost. There's the head. They're looking at David Lee and they followed him here from work."

I don't know if the ghost followed me from work, or whether it was at the complex already. I do work at a haunted hospital, however. David D. could not accept the fact that a ghost flew by and ruined his brother's picture. David tried to tell me the picture was a result of Mitch bumping into his computer while developing the photograph. (That's a bunch of bologna.)

Danny, who worked for the county, lives in an apartment complex in Campbell. Back in 1999, I gave Danny a picture of the ghost coming through the bathroom door of our room aboard *The Queen Mary*. That night, he brought the picture home and showed it to his wife while they were in the kitchen. Danny had left the photograph on the kitchen table. Later that evening, while they were watching television in the living room, Danny heard the sound of someone in the kitchen washing dishes. Danny asked his wife if her sister was washing dishes. His wife's sister was asleep at the time. Danny decided to get up and take a look in the kitchen. As soon as Danny turned the light on, the noise stopped. The incident never happened again. Had the ghost of the Queen Mary stopped by to clean up before the next voyage?

A HAUNTED BUILDING

A building on Hamilton Avenue and San Thomas Expressway is rumored to be haunted. A language school and a security firm occupy the building. A couple of guards, who work for Securitas, had no knowledge of their building being haunted, but they've heard ghost stories from co-workers. Most of the paranormal activity occurs at night. Other guards have seen ghosts, shadows, and objects moving on their own. Sometimes, they find something broken without an explanation. It appears that the ghosts at this location are quite secure with security…

THE LATE GREAT GAS LIGHTER THEATRE

The building where The Gas Lighter Theatre in Campbell was located, was originally The Bank of Campbell, built in 1923. After World War II ended, the building was turned into a theatre, in the late 40s. I had no idea the theatre was haunted when I randomly went inside to ask if they had ghosts.

Susan was working that day, and according to her, visitors frequently see ghosts, mostly in the balcony. At least three ghosts haunt the theatre, including an old man and a boy. The ghost of the old man is thought to be an ex- employee who ran the film projector when a movie theatre operated in the building. The ghost of the child is a boy, whose name is either Harold or Howard Harleson. I'll call him Harold. While he and his friends were swimming at the nearby creek, where my friends and I used to swim, he accidentally hit his head while diving into the creek.

My assistant and I returned to the theatre to see Wendy as a star in a play. She knew all about the ghosts at The Gas Lighter, and her Sylvia Brown book was sitting stately on the counter to show her interest in the world beyond. It seems that back in the 1940s, a man who ran the projector used to let Harold and his friends into the movie for free. A Campbell newspaper published a story about the ghosts at the theatre, but stories and rumors based on Harold's origin were not completely factual. One day, a woman called on the telephone because she wanted everybody to get the story straight. In the background, her husband was heard saying, "They don't need to know everything." The woman's husband was one of Harold's four friends, from back in the 40s. The woman insisted on spilling the beans and revealed more information.

After Harold drowned, his friends avoided the theatre because it reminded them of him. Eventually, they went back to watch a movie and were sitting in the balcony watching the film. They turned around and saw the ghost of Harold sitting a few rows behind them. I think they were scared and ran out of the theatre.

Wendy did go to Oak Hill Cemetery to look for Harold's grave which is number 137. She was unable to find it. The place is enormous.

Alise, Susan's ten-year-old daughter, saw three ghosts, including the ghost of an elderly woman. Wendy saw shadows and heard the sounds of footsteps on stage, when no one was on or near the stage. Wendy was using the ladies room in the upstairs balcony. She was the only person up there and she heard the sound of a man urinating in the men's room, which was vacant at the time. One evening, Wendy and her co-worker were in the upstairs restroom. They both witnessed a ghost's hand come over the top the stall; then the ghost dematerialized.

One of Wendy's scariest nights at the theatre was the night when the Ghost Trackers organization spent the night investigating the premises—though nothing substantial happened. That could be contributed by the creepy circumstances in general. Still, Wendy no longer goes upstairs by herself.

She did bring me upstairs and allowed me to take a picture of her standing in the balcony. Ghosts were seen on the stairway that led to the balcony. An actress named Claire, who worked at the Gas Lighter, came over to converse with me, telling me that she encountered the ghost of Harold while she was near the balcony. The ghost was standing at the top of the stairs tossing a ball up in the air and catching it.

Wendy was working in the theatre by herself and she was listening to the music of rap star Eminem on her boom box. The ghost didn't want to hear it. All of a sudden, Wendy heard footsteps above her in the balcony. The footsteps sounded as if they belonged to an agitated person. Wendy decided to say, "Screw that." She turned the music up louder. The footsteps in the balcony above her became louder as the ghost stomped its way around the balcony. The ghost did not quit stomping around until Wendy turned the music off.

On the other side of the ghost issue, the man who owned the theatre said, "I have been here for thirty years and I have not seen any ghosts in here."

Unfortunately, The Gas Lighter Theatre no longer exists. But, the building is being renovated to become a night club and will include an elevator, along with a new second level. On August 8, 2007, Steve and a crew of his friends were working at the building, helping to clear everything out. It was daytime and I asked Steve if I could take some pictures inside the building. We went inside; I started taking photos, and I noticed right away that a lot of orbs were appearing for my camera. Some of the pictures taken in the front of the theatre had little or no orbs. The back of the theatre was loaded. I told Steve about the orbs and he rounded up four of his friends for a picture. I took the picture and showed it to Steve and the other four. There were orbs in the picture with them.

The five of them came together for another picture, and I have never seen so many orbs. The orbs voluntarily came together for the picture. I could not hear a sound from the orbs, nor did I feel any weird vibes inside the theatre. Nick is the owner of the building, and according to him, the bill of sale states that the building is haunted.

The Gas Lighter crew among a sea of orbs at the theatre. August 6, 2007.

CONCLUSION

San Jose has a surplus of haunted places, and there are many ghost stories beyond what I've touched upon here.

For those in search of ghosts, I highly recommend this fine city. Some of the ghosts will know you came to see them, and they might appear in a picture, if you bring your camera with you.

Visitors from near and far will be welcomed at most of the haunted places I've mentioned in this book. And not to worry; the chances of being harmed by a ghost in San Jose are slim and there's a good chance if you search hard enough, you'll find a haunted place that even I don't know about!

Good luck on your quest for ghosts!

BIBLIOGRAPHY

Boulland, Michael. *Whoppers and Ghostly Tales from Rancho Santa Theresa*. San Jose, California. Santa Theresa Press. 1996.

Fokard, Claire (Managing Editor). *Guinness Book of World Records*. London. Bantam Books, 2004.

Guiley, Rosemary Ellen. *Encyclopedia of Ghosts and Spirits*. New York. Checkmark Books, 2000.

Guthertz, Alvin T. "How a Publicity Stunt Turned up a Ghost." *Psychic World*, 1976.

Hauck, Dennis W. *Haunted Places*. Bergenfield, New Jersey. Penguin Books, 1986.

Winer, Richard. Osbourne, Nancy. *Haunted Houses*. New York. 1980, 33-49.

Senate, Richard. *Ghosts of the Haunted Coast*. Channel Islands. Pathfinder Publishing. 1986, 1999.

Shadowlands.net/places/california2.htm.

Smith, Barbara. *Ghost Stories of California*. Edmonton, Canada. Lone Pine Books. 2000

Stroble, Bill. "Think You Have Uninvited Guests?" *San Jose News*. October 29, 1981.

VMC Historical Society Newsletter. October 2006.